CAREER PATHS:

A Guide to Jobs

in

Criminal Justice

Second Edition

Gordon M. Armstrong
Georgia Southern University, Statesboro, Georgia

Shelia C. Armstrong
The Justice Research Association, Hilton Head Island, South Carolina

Prentice Hall, Upper Saddle River, New Jersey 07458

Director of Production: *Bruce Johnson*
Acquisitions Editor: *Neil Marquardt*
Production Supervisor: *Mary Carnis*
Buyer: *Ed O'Dougherty*
Production Editor: *Denise Brown*
Cover Design: *Miguel Ortiz*
Marketing Manager: *Frank Mortimer, Jr.*

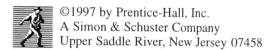

Printed in the United States of America

10   9   8   7   6   5   4   3   2   1

ISBN 0-13-741513-3

Prentice-Hall International (UK) Limited, *London*
Prentice-Hall of Australia Pty. Limited, *Sydney*
Prentice-Hall Canada Inc., *Toronto*
Prentice-Hall Hispanoamericana, S.A., *Mexico*
Prentice-Hall of India Private Limited, *New Delhi*
Prentice-Hall of Japan, Inc., *Tokyo*
Simon & Schuster Asia Pte. Ltd., *Singapore*
Editora Prentice-Hall do Brasil, Ltda., *Rio de Janeiro*

For

Warren Conner Armstrong

and

Joseph Paul Cope

All the inspiration we need

Contents

Acknowledgments

We are grateful to Neil Marquardt, Acquisitions Editor at Prentice Hall Career and Technology, for the opportunity to produce this work. Though we're not too sure if he's a real person or just a voice on an answering machine.

And, as always, Frank Schmalleger's incessant phone calls continuously encouraged and motivated us, and his creative ideas were tremendously helpful in the collection of information and the development of content.

Our thanks to you both.

Shelia C. Armstrong
Gordon M. Armstrong

INTRODUCTION

IT'S <u>STILL</u> A MESS!

Recently released crime rate data show heartening statistical reductions in some reporting categories, but crime remains a major problem in American society. Polls continuously rank crime at or near the top of citizens' concerns. Incidents of domestic terrorism are escalating, with mind-numbing tallies of dead and wounded. Violent crime continues to fill nightly newscasts with heart-wrenching footage of the victims of bombings and shootings. Weeping survivors and stunned neighbors still wonder how such terrible things could have happened to them, and newscasters report the mayhem in the same bored voices they use to announce ball scores.

Law-abider and lawbreaker alike still devour the daily reports with relish. Television programs with titles like *Cops* and *America's Most Wanted* maintain high ratings by providing vicarious thrills for Dirty Harry Callahan-wannabes. There's even a thriving videotape market for those who wish to collect these disturbing portrayals of the downside of American life for repeated viewing.

Youthful prisoners still arrogantly flash peace signs at news team mini-cams while strutting into court or jail. When ultimately released, they often return to hero's welcomes in "the hood," and are afforded greater status for having cycled through the system.

Prisons remain grossly overcrowded. Many inmates are released after having served only a fifth of their sentence—or less. Some commit new crimes, only to be arrested, tried and sentenced again before expiration of the *original* sentence from which they were released early! Criminals continue to laugh at the system while accepting jail sentences over probation, because doing so gets them turned loose so much sooner.

Yes, it still seems a hopeless mess. But we continue to believe that, while these seemingly impossible problems may never be eliminated, they are manageable. And we continue to see you as the key to solving these and future criminal justice problems as you bring to the field your fresh perspectives and ideas for solving them. As hopeless as conditions may appear, none of these problems is insurmountable.

OPPORTUNITY!

So, again we ask—what's in it for you? Wealth? Fame? Cushy working conditions, short hours, long lunches, and lots of perks?

Not hardly! But tremendous opportunities <u>do exist</u> for meaningful, rewarding careers as criminal justice practitioners and researchers. Federal, state, and local government agencies, and burgeoning private agencies, provide thousands of opportunities for those seeking a career in this important field. These positions will provide comfortable incomes, essential benefits packages, and reasonable assurance of job security. They will also provide great personal satisfaction from the knowledge that what you are doing enriches society.

We often hear students and others comment that they are avoiding criminal justice as a career consideration because they "don't want to be a cop." We will dispel the idea that police work is all that is available in this dynamic career field.

This revised booklet has been retitled from the original *Career Paths: A Guide to Jobs in Federal Law Enforcement*, and its scope has been expanded to provide you with general information about career opportunities throughout the criminal justice field. Good jobs await you at all levels within the criminal justice system. Each level of the system—federal, state, local, or the private sector—presents its own set of advantages and disadvantages. We will point out some considerations that you may have overlooked.

This booklet <u>will not</u> answer all your who-what-when-where-how and why questions about finding a criminal justice job. Its aim is simply to get you headed in the right direction by providing general information about:

a. Well-known (e.g.: FBI) and lesser-known (e.g.: Bureau of Engraving and Printing) federal agencies, and the criminal justice career opportunities they offer.

b. Criminal justice career opportunities in state and local agencies that perform functions similar to those of their federal counterparts.

c. Criminal justice positions unique to particular states or regions.

d. Criminal justice career opportunities in private sector agencies.

e. Criminal justice research opportunities.

f. Resume preparation.

g. Job-search tactics.

h. Completion of applications and related documents.

i. Do's and don'ts about interview preparation and performance.

j. Quickly establishing your credibility during those nervous first days in your new job.

k. Use of such technologically advanced resources as the Internet (for finding job openings), fax communications, and presentation software.

Our goal is to give you information and ideas to help get your job search moving, and to give you an edge as you compete for available positions. This is not a comprehensive telephone directory of criminal justice agencies. It does provide basic point-of-contact data for many organizations, but it is by no means a complete listing. Our intent is to serve as a starting point in the process of narrowing this wide-open career field down to a manageable number of options. We identify positions and agencies about which you may have been unaware, and present some common-sense advice on steps to take and mistakes to avoid as you pursue your new job.

Chapters 1 and 2 discuss various specialty areas within the criminal justice system, typical jobs within each area, and resources for obtaining information about career opportunities within this field.

The all-important resume is the focus of Chapter 3. Strategies regarding length and content are discussed, and some typical mistakes are highlighted.

Chapter 4 discusses the interview, including some sound ideas for preparation, advice on things to do or avoid during the interview itself, and appropriate actions to take as follow-ups after completing an interview.

Chapter 5 addresses things to consider when you've won the job and are trying to establish your credibility during your first days on the job.

Appendix A contains general data about positions available within the various federal agencies. Addresses and telephone numbers for listed agencies are provided.

Appendix B provides samples of criminal justice pages on the World Wide Web.

Appendix C provides helpful suggestions pertaining to completion and processing of the federal application forms (Standard Form 171 and Optional Form 612). Much of the advice in the section can be applied to the various state forms as well, and will benefit you by focusing your efforts and helping you avoid common administrative errors that might derail your application.

Appendix D provides samples of a fully detailed resume, as well as a shorter, more concise version.

Appendices E, F and G are extracts of various federal pay tables.

Appendix H provides sample letters for use at various stages of the job search process.

Appendix I presents a sample of a properly completed Application for Federal Employment (SF-171).

You've selected a great career field, and we wish you good luck in your pursuit of the *right* job for you. The opportunities are out there—go get 'em!

1

Law Enforcement, Courts, Corrections, or Research?

You know, for people seeking a career in the criminal justice field, narrowing down the choices can be a mind boggling experience. There is an incredible array of options to choose from, and each one has much to offer.

Take law enforcement, for example. You can be everything from a hard-nosed street cop, a la *NYPD Blue*, to a child protective services investigator, or a fishing industry investigator for the U.S. Fish and Wildlife Service. Your duties can range from front-line combat in the war on crime to behind-the-scenes document scrutiny in an effort to track down laundered drug money. You want sweat, grime, rotating shift work, long periods of boring routine, and occasional episodes of adrenalin-overdose and high danger? It's out there. Keyboards, monitors, and 9-to-5? That's out there, too.

How about court work? There are bailiff, court administrator, docket manager, legal stenographer and transcriber, pre-sentencing investigator, legal clerk, and innumerable other support positions available in approximately 17,000 general, limited, and appellate courts throughout the nation. Jurisdictional opportunities range across the federal, state, and local levels. You can travel throughout a judicial district, or stay put in your own home town.

With today's astounding—and rising—incarceration rates, corrections is a growth industry unto itself. Jails, prisons, probation and parole offices, and a myriad of community correctional and counseling facilities across the country need manpower in every imaginable position, from warden to drug rehab counselor to prisoner intake and classification specialist. Community corrections programs need talented administrators with education or experience in the criminal justice system.

Unique opportunities await those with special talents or training, too. Combine your skills as an artist with your interest in criminal investigation and become a forensic artist. Are you good with a camera or video recorder? Crime scene photographers are an essential member of every effective investigative team. Lab technicians, polygraph operators, chemists, forensic scientists, identification technicians, ballistics experts, document examiners, serologists, arson specialists—we could fill more than a few pages with a list of specialized positions that support investigators at every level.

Opportunities abound for those inclined to combine criminal justice interests with a desire to serve in one of the armed forces. Crime exists in the military, too, and the various branches each have their own justice system to keep staffed.

If a career in a governmental agency just doesn't suit you, the entire private security industry is available. Credit investigators, loss prevention specialists, security detectives, guards, alarm technicians, private police, and security managers are in demand. In this age of escalating domestic terrorism, personal security specialists have little difficulty finding steady employment. Retailers, industrialists, landlords, and scores of other business managers are snapping up skilled security people in an effort to reduce losses to theft or pilferage and reduce exposure to liability resulting from physical harm suffered by clients and visitors.

And what about research? Well-known agencies such as the National Institute of Justice and the Bureau of Justice Statistics have continuous need for qualified researchers, but they certainly aren't your only options. Research opportunities exist in private facilities such as the Rand Corporation or the Justice Research Association, as well as in educational institutions in almost every state. The national crime epidemic has spawned a major effort to identify causes and develop effective responses as government at every level seeks to protect the public. Criminal justice researchers are needed throughout the system to collect, analyze, and interpret data that may yield important clues in the search for solutions.

Are you getting the idea that there is more out there than you might have originally thought? There is far more to the criminal justice field than just walking a beat or guarding a cell block. The career possibilities are widely varied, and each carries with it the special rewards of security and a sense of fulfillment from having met a truly critical need in society.

The trick now, of course, is to determine career considerations that are important to you. By default, that will screen out many positions and help you trim this list of options down to a manageable size. No one other than yourself can know what factors about particular job options are either attractive or absolutely out of the question to you. Each of us is unique in our tastes and preferences. For example, some think they would wither in an office setting, while others couldn't imagine routinely functioning in the street. And if you can't stand the thought of staring into a microscope for a major portion of each work day, you'd better give up the idea of being a forensic pathologist.

It is obvious that you must make an honest assessment of your personal likes and dislikes at the outset of your career search. As previously stated, such an analysis almost

2

automatically eliminates many positions from consideration. Once you've narrowed the field somewhat, then you should begin factoring in other elements, such as:

- Your willingness to travel and remain away from home overnight. If that idea doesn't appeal to you, abandon the idea of being a U.S. Marshal, a U.S. Customs Agent, or similar jobs.

- Your willingness to work on rotating shifts. Most police officers and correctional officers are subject to this type of scheduling.

- Your willingness to relocate. Many federal agencies routinely rotate their personnel to field offices around the country.

- Your preference for indoor or outdoor work. If you're a computer geek by nature, and you wouldn't go camping on a bet, don't pursue a position as a Border Patrol Agent with the U.S. Immigration and Naturalization Service.

- Personal characteristics you possess or lack, such as patience, interpersonal communication skills, or a quick temper. If you're a frenetic Type-A personality, don't seek a job which entails conducting surveillance of suspects. Those of you who lack the ability to communicate effectively should give up the notion of being a polygraph operator or interrogator. And you hot-tempered folks should avoid jobs as correctional officers, where the people you'll spend your entire workday with everyday thrive on provoking guards as if it were a sporting event.

In other words, use common sense. Limit your search to jobs that fit your nature, and reject those that cause you to mentally flinch at the thought of working in them.

Even if you cut out 75 or 80 percent of the potential jobs from consideration, there will still be thousands of possibilities that remain. Thousands? Yes, easily that many. The next task is to find them. So, on to Chapter 2, where you'll find plenty of information on how to locate the best opportunities.

2

Where Are the Jobs, and How Do I Find Them?

Those thousands of jobs we spoke of in Chapter 1 can be found in any village, town, city, county, and state. There are openings at the federal and international levels. They are available in business and industry, the military, on campuses, in hospitals, in high-rise office buildings, banks, hotels, or on the highways.

Yeah, we all know where they are—but *where are they?* Not as in "the location in which they are performed," but as in "how do I get information about them, and where do I apply?"

As recently as ten years ago, finding out about job openings was largely a matter of luck. Your Aunt Ethel mentioned that you were looking for work to a woman at church whose brother-in-law played softball with a guy who happened to be looking for, etc., etc. As strange as it may seem, such scenarios were not at all uncommon, and many careers began on just such a fluke.

All too often, however, genuinely qualified candidates never got the opportunity to compete for jobs because they didn't learn the job was available until it had already been filled with a less qualified applicant. The agency lost out because they had to settle for lower quality. The best qualified person lost out by not getting the job. The only winner was the newly hired person who would not have won the job in fair competition with the better qualified candidate.

Today, things are a bit different. It's still an awfully competitive world out there, and it takes aggressive research and tenacity to locate and secure a good position. But as a result of advances in technology, the research part of the job search has become outrageously easy.

We're talking Internet here, folks, and the World Wide Web. If you haven't learned to use them yet, you'd better. In less than an hour, you can find out about job openings in every major sub-field of criminal justice, and in every imaginable location. Even international openings are cited here! And it's not just a simple announcement of a position's availability. This is comprehensive information. Applicant qualifications; educational requirements; duty descriptions; salary ranges; application deadlines; names, addresses, voice and fax telephone numbers, and e-mail addresses of the contact points at the hiring agencies—it's incredible!

Do we sound enthused? Boy, are we! This is a gold mine of information for the job seeker, and we are thrilled to see it.

The beauty of this resource is the currency of the data. Agencies input their announcements almost daily, and withdraw announcements of filled positions very quickly, which keeps you from wasting time going after jobs that are already filled. The national scope is invaluable, too. Tired of the gnats in Savannah, Georgia? That opening in Minot, North Dakota, might be right up your alley. Sick of shoveling snow? C'mon down and shovel all these gnats in Savannah. (You can replace the guy who went to Minot!) Get the idea? It's the "now-ness" of the information that makes it so valuable.

It would be almost impossible to list all of the databases that are available. There are so many of them, and more are added so often, that it would be silly to try. But we're going to tour a few of them to give you an idea of the dynamic nature of this resource.

We must state at the outset, however, that the tours will be somewhat restricted by copyright limitations. The people who manage these sites are doing all of us a great service. We don't want to do them any disservice, nor do we want to repay their efforts by disrespecting their wishes. In fact, we applaud their ingenuity, their dedication, and their commitment to public service.

That said, let's take a look at one of the most popular sites, Cecil Greek's *Criminal Justice Links*. It's available at http://www.stpt./usf.edu/~greek/cj.html, and it's awesome! The home page for this site is at Sample 1, Appendix B. Note the vast array of subject areas for which he maintains database links. National listings of job openings are accessible under many of the headings, such as the following:

- Federal Criminal Justice Agencies.

- International Criminal Justice Sources.

- Police Agencies and Resources.

- The Courts: Due Process and Civil Liberties.

- Prisons and the Death Penalty.

A review of the material provided under two of the headings clearly demonstrates the great power of this resource. If you click on *Police Agencies and Resources*, you get a menu called *Law Enforcement Agencies on the Web* (sample 2, Appendix B) that offers job listings under the following headings:

- College and University Police Departments.

- State Law Enforcement Agencies.

- Municipal Police Departments and County Sheriffs.

- Military Police Departments.

- Police Agencies Outside the United States.

- Miscellaneous Law Enforcement Programs.

Click *Prisons and the Death Penalty* and you get a menu that includes an entry for the *Corrections Connection Network*. When you go to it, select *Job Opportunities*, which opens a page entitled *Job Openings Across the Nation*. That's a state-by-state listing of openings in the corrections field that even includes a sub-page called the *Database of Job Seekers* where people who are looking for a corrections job can post their resumes.

Wow—what a resource! Cecil Greek is extraordinarily popular on the Web, and rightfully so. His material is timely, comprehensive, and accurate. We strongly recommend this site.

Another great site is maintained by Boston Police Officer James Meredith. It's the *Police Officer's Internet Directory*, and we rate it right up there with Cecil Greek. Access this site at http://www.officer.com., and you'll be glad you did. Its numerous directories of value to law enforcement job seekers include, among others, the:

- Complete Directory of Law Enforcement Agencies.

- Corrections Officer Resource Directory.

- Criminal Justice Resource Directory.

- Law Enforcement Employment Directory.

- Police Specialized Units Resource Directory.

Employment and *Jobs* headings under some of these titles lead you to national listings of law enforcement openings. Jim Meredith deserves high praise for his outstanding efforts. The highest praise you can give him is to use the site, and we recommend that you do.

Glenn's Law Enforcement Web Pages are a virtual cornucopia of law enforcement job information. Found at http://www.dimensional.com/~glenn976/law/employment, the pages are maintained by Glenn B. Howell, smartly arranged in such categories as:

- Continual Hiring Employment Page.

- Current Openings Employment Page.

- Agencies On-Line with Job Pages.

Under each heading, Glenn categorizes the announcements by job title. The entries that follow are actual job announcements from agencies around the country. This, too, is an outstanding site.

In addition to these general databases, many public agencies have jumped on the Web. Appendix B, contains the following samples of such public agency Web sites:

- Sample 3 is *Employment Opportunities at the Lawton Police Department*, at http://www.sirinet.net/~lawtonpd/employ.htm. This is a comprehensive document that answers all your questions about joining the Lawton, Oklahoma, Police Department.

- *DEA Special Agent*, located at http://www.usdoj.gov/dea/employ/tocg.htm, is Sample 4. This home page contains menu selections that provide comprehensive information about qualifications, salary and benefits, and hiring procedures.

- At http://www.dimensional.com/~glenn976/law/employment/jcsd.htm is the home page of the Jefferson County, Colorado, Sheriff's Department (Sample 5). This sample announces that the department is not currently hiring.

- Sample 6 is Florida Attorney General Bob Butterworth's excellent home page at http://legal.firn.edu/. Note the *Job Opportunities* heading on the right.

- Lastly, Sample 7 is the Illinois Criminal Justice Information Authority's home page, found at http://www.icjia.org/. Included in this sample is the listing of openings displayed when you click the heading *Employment Opportunities*.

The information available on the Web is almost more than you can sort through. We urge you, however, to dive right in and soak it up. Don't be afraid of this resource. If you lack the technical know-how, ask for help. An excellent source is your local librarian. Almost all of them are Web-Wizards, and they're willing and eager to make you a wizard, too.

3

The Resume

What exactly is a resume, anyway? Essentially, it is a brief summary of a person's qualifications and experiences, and it is usually prepared by someone who is seeking a position of some kind.

And what is its purpose? That answer is a bit trickier. Some say it serves to get you hired. We believe its real value is to get you interviewed, which just might get you hired.

There are as many ideas about the "right" way to prepare a resume as there are people who prepare them. And what is the "right" way? Because it such an intensely personal document, you are the sole judge of that.

The resume lets you present what you think is important about yourself in your own words. It gives the reader a sense of you that does not come across from a fill-in-the-blank application form. Just as each of us prefers a particular clothing style, certain kinds of shoes, or a unique haircut, we all have our own idea of the image of ourselves we want to create with our resume. Once you decide what that image is, it becomes a simple matter to play up the things that will enhance your image while downplaying anything that may diminish it.

There are some general rules that should guide you, and we offer here some advice about things to consider as you create this written image of yourself. Of course, common sense has to be your first guide. You probably don't want to use profanity in your resume, for example, or write in a convoluted literary style.

With that in mind, consider the content of the resume. Basic information such as your name, address, telephone number, and e-mail address (if any) is essential, of course. After all, you certainly want to make it easy for them to contact you, don't you? Additionally, you should cite your educational credentials, your work experience and, if space permits, volunteer experience.

But avoid excessive detail. We recommend omitting your social security number, birth date, references, height, weight, religious affiliation, the names of your wife, children, and pets, your hobbies, shoe size, date of appendectomy, and other such data. (And please, do not put the useless statement "References available upon request." *Of course* you'll provide them a list of references if they want one. You're competing for a job; are you going to say "no" if they ask?!?)

Why leave all that stuff out? First, it just makes your resume that much more difficult to read. Second, if you answer all their questions about you in the resume, there will be nothing left to talk about in an interview. The odds are, then, that an invitation to interview won't be extended.

Let's take a minute to look at the situation facing you when you submit a resume. The act of submitting the document normally takes place in response to the announcement of an available position for which you want to be considered. You can assume that you won't be the only respondent to the announcement, so your first objective is to get your resume noticed out of all the resumes received. In some cases, that may be a pile of resumes numbering in the hundreds. Obviously, then, there must be something noteworthy about yours if you hope to be culled out from the also-rans. And believe this—a clean, efficient resume is noteworthy!

A couple of facts can guide you here. First, the human resources worker doing the initial review is just a normal human being who is faced with the rather overwhelming task of picking out the best of the lot. In an ideal world, that worker would read every word of every resume received, then use some evaluative process to rank each candidate. S/He would then forward the top ten or so for consideration by his/her superiors.

But this isn't an ideal world, and human nature frequently drives the process. Often, that very human human resource worker will resort to the most expedient method for trimming the pile down to manageable size by creating two piles from the first pile. Pile number one will contain all of the one- or two-page, easily digestible resumes. The second pile will contain all the resumes with three or more pages. Naturally, the length of the resumes in the second pile makes them far more time-consuming to read and evaluate, while the brevity of the resumes in the first pile makes them comparatively easy to work with.

From your perspective, the response is obvious: keep your resume at one page if at all possible. Some tricks for doing so include reducing the font size to 10-point, and reducing the top, bottom, and side margins to .75 inches. (You can even take the margins down to .50 inches if necessary, but that's pushing it.) Most word processing programs allow you to customize page setups, so play with it a little until you find the setup that works best with your information.

Some resume preparers recommend the use of specially colored paper to make your resume stand out from the ordinary pile of white papers. They offer various shades of ivory, off-white, pale yellow, blue, green, tan, gray—the possibilities are endless. It is our opinion that such advice is more to the benefit of the resume preparer than it is to you, the client, serving primarily as a ploy to enable them to sell you a more expensive line of paper.

Most organizations are conservative and inclined toward traditionally accepted business practices. Today's businesses and public agencies usually use white paper for external correspondence. Non-traditional coloration on correspondence they receive tends to put them off, causing them to see the applicant as a nonconformist. Frankly, when you are trying to convince them that they should hire you because you'll fit into their work force, nonconformist actions confuse your signals.

A well prepared resume tells experienced human resources managers an awful lot about you. The manner in which you present information displays your efficiency, maturity, and professionalism. Here are some general hints:

- Use professional language that is simple and direct.

- Don't use nine-dollar words that just confuse your message.

- Stay away from slang or fad terms. Your resume is no place to be cute.

- NO profanity!

- When listing your record of experience, don't leave unexplained time gaps.

- Give sufficient detail to reduce or eliminate questions, but not so much detail as to make it difficult to read.

- Avoid gimmickry. Bold fonts or underlining that appropriately sets off job titles or categories within the resume is fine, but resist the temptation to use italics or other font enhancements to emphasize an entry you want noticed.

- Don't embellish! Be completely honest regarding scope of responsibilities or types of duties performed in past positions. If you start playing with numbers, you may find yourself tripped up during an interview. You will be absolutely dead in the water if your integrity comes under suspicion.

- Before printing the resume, use the spell-check function on your word processor one last time. If it has a grammar-check function, use that, too.

- Read and re-read your resume, and have another person read it, too. Look specifically to ensure that dates don't overlap or have gaps; that the information about work experience follows a logical reverse-order sequence from your current position back to your first job; that address and telephone data are accurate; and that the general appearance of the document is clean and uncluttered.

Now comes the question of length. Applicants just completing their education and seeking entry-level management positions typically have short work histories and should find it easy to prepare a concise resume. Normally, the longer you've been in the work force, the more information you have to include in your resume. One of our colleagues has a 35-year work history, more than 12 years of education beyond high school, and extensive records of professional affiliation, community service, and publication. He has two resumes prepared. The long form runs 14 pages; the short one is not quite two pages.

How does he decide which to submit? For general solicitation responses, he submits the short form. If that sparks interest and an invitation to complete an application or be interviewed, he either encloses the long form with the application or brings it along to the interview. (By the way, he usually brings a prepared list of references to hand over to the interviewer, too. That's an excellent technique for displaying your thoroughness and professionalism.)

Your personal circumstance, and the particulars of the job announcement to which you are responding, will normally dictate which format would be best. Again, however, this is one of the calls you have to make as a matter of image projection.

Lastly, if you submit the resume by mail or some other delivery means, do not fold it. Put it in a large cardboard envelope to protect it from being mutilated during transport. And don't just send it by itself. Prepare a cover letter (see Sample Letter 3 at Appendix H), and attach the resume as an enclosure to the letter.

The bottom line on resume preparation is this: keep it clean, clear, concise, and complete. Be as brief as possible without excluding truly important details. Make it a statement of your professionalism, and it will open doors for you.

4

The Interview

If there is any one area of the job search process that demands the application of common sense more than any other, it is the interview. You can prepare a dynamic resume, then make it all the way through the difficult initial screening process, and end up blowing the whole thing when you get in front of the decision makers.

How can you keep that from happening? Well, there are no guarantees. Sometimes your personality just does not click with the person doing the interview, and despite your best efforts, things don't work out. That's human nature. But there are some things you can do, and others you can avoid, to increase your probability of success.

The following suggestions—all of which are rooted in common sense—will give you an edge during this typically nerve-wracking process:

- Relax. Exhibit a poised, confident manner that signals maturity and competence. But watch out! It is easy to appear arrogant or cocky, and those aren't the signals you want to send.

- Use the restroom before you report for the interview. Check your hair, clothes, and shoes. If you ate before arrival, it's probably a good idea to brush your teeth. (You lose points quickly for lettuce in your teeth!)

- Don't be late. Tardiness is one of the best ways to blow an opportunity real fast. Be smart about it and get there early. It is far better to arrive well in advance of the appointed hour than to show up even one minute late. Arriving early gives you plenty of time to find a place to park, run down change for the meter, use the restroom, or do any of the million other unforeseen things that can crop up, and still get to the specific office where you're supposed to be in plenty of time

- Grooming counts. If you gnaw your nails, stop. Comb your hair neatly, wear clean, pressed clothing, and shine those shoes. The first impression you make will be visual. If it's a negative impression, the entire interview will be an uphill battle for you.

- Remember that you are trying to demonstrate how well you'll fit into the nice, quiet, conservative environment of the interviewer's agency or business. While the latest styles in clothing, especially fad styles (remember parachute pants?) might look good in the local clubs, they don't play well in corporate America. Prospective employers prefer people who display moderation and the tendency to fit in. Avoid dramatic makeup or jewelry, too.

- Avoid smoking. It has become an unpopular habit that is best not displayed during the interview visit.

- Be conscious of your language; don't use profanity, and avoid slang.

- Rehearse. Yes, rehearse, just as though you have a script for the interview. Ask a friend or family member to role-play the interview with you. Have them ask the sorts of questions you might expect (e.g., "How did you learn about this position?"; "Briefly describe your experience related to this position."), as well as those curve-ball questions that seem to come out of nowhere and catch you off guard (e.g., "How would you handle a situation involving a romantic liaison between two subordinates, one of whom is married and is the direct supervisor of the other?"). Develop a relaxed delivery that portrays confidence and maturity.

- Slow down. Speak in measured tones at a moderate pace. No one can follow your answer when you use a machine-gun delivery style that sounds like this: "YesIhaveexperienceinbudgetformulationpresentationanddefenseinfactIheldrespo nsibilityforthosefunctionsinamultisectionalsettingatAcmeSecurityServices."

- Don't just blurt out the first response that pops into your head as you hear each question. Pause for a moment and gather your thoughts. Formulate an answer that addresses all elements of the question.

- Keep your answers brief. If you find yourself rambling on for three or four minutes at each question, you're babbling. They don't want to hear babble!

- Look your questioner directly in the eye as you are being asked a question. If you are not sure you understand, or you simply do not hear the question, ask him/her to repeat it.

- If there is more than one interviewer present, look at each one in turn as you are answering the questions. Do so in a manner that is appropriate to normal group conversations.

- In formulating your answers, try to find ways to tell them how you can contribute to their operation. Don't just spout off a litany of past experiences; they can read about those in your resume.

- Be conscious of any nervous habits you have, and control them. Don't bounce your foot up and down on its toes at a speed reminiscent of a hummingbird's wings. Don't crack your knuckles. Get rid of your gum before you report for the interview.

In a nutshell: don't do dumb things! Be relaxed, charming, gracious, appropriately deferential, and courteous. Use the manners Mom taught you, and use them with everyone from the receptionist on up to the senior person you meet. You want to make them like you, and common courtesy is the key to achieving that goal.

Remember to follow up the interview with thank you letters to each person you met during your visit. It's astounding how this very effective method of selling one's self is so routinely overlooked. Use it!

It's best to prepare thank you letters at the first opportunity, while things are still fresh in your memory. Standard appreciative comments are appropriate, and it is also a great idea to remind them of some positive element of the interview that you want to highlight. (See the second paragraph of Sample Letter 4 in Appendix H.)

Finally, we recommend mailing follow-up letters as soon as possible after the interview, while you are still fresh in their memories. Timely receipt of such a letter may be just the impetus they need to opt for you if their decision has boiled down to the last two or three candidates.

Common sense, courtesy, poise, and confidence are the keys to a successful interview. Use them effectively, and the experience will be less stressful and more productive.

5

Those Nervous First Days

Congratulations! You've won the job you went after and, of course, you are filled with excitement, pride, and anticipation. Now you desperately want to quickly establish yourself as a worthwhile member of your new team.

One of the first things you must do is get control of your own enthusiasm. Recognize that you are probably not going to go into your new position and solve all of your boss' problems right from the get-go. And guess what? S/He isn't looking for you to do that, either. Bosses don't want someone to come in and take over; they simply want someone to fit in. They want you to do the job for which you were hired right from the start, and they want your arrival to be as minimally disruptive as possible.

Common sense prevails here, too. Read everything you can find about what your new agency or business does, and particularly what role your department plays, before you show up for your first day. The more you know about what it is the group does, the faster you'll begin contributing to their efforts.

Typically, you will be faced with an initial transition period that will entail being trained about the peculiarities of your new position. You'll learn the what, where, and how of your new duties. You will also be introduced to those with whom you will routinely interact, including members of your new agency and representatives of agencies or businesses with which your agency has dealings. Pay attention. Be courteous, respectful, and appropriately deferential. Ask smart questions, but don't ask questions simply for the sake of saying something. Take lots of notes, and remember that your first duty is to learn, learn, learn.

Remember, too, that you are now in the work force, and you are expected to produce work in exchange for the pay you receive. Do not be surprised if you are given tasks or projects that you are expected to accomplish on your own. After you've been there awhile, you will probably recognize that your initial taskings were relatively simple. Bosses will often test new hires by giving them simple requirements to gauge their initiative, purposefulness, and sense of duty.

If you find yourself in this situation, try to get the job done on your own. Do appropriate research, then formulate your solution to the task. ("Appropriate research" does not mean simply bugging your coworkers with incessant "how do I ..." questions. Most organizations have published guidance for accomplishing most of the things they do. Learn to be self-sufficient. If you can't find it in the books, then ask.) Once you've developed what you think is a solid response, stifle your urge to act long enough to float your solution past your boss in the form of a recommendation. This gives him/her the opportunity to catch things you might have overlooked, or possibly to bless your solution before enactment—with the side benefit to you of being impressed by your performance!

It is critical to establish your judgment, reliability, and competence as early as possible. Gaining your boss' confidence early on makes life so much more pleasant. When you are considered reliable by those who supervise your work, you gain independence and autonomy. No one likes to have someone looking over their shoulder all the time. Do your initial jobs well, and your boss will quickly decide that you don't need babysitting. After all, s/he is busy, and wants very much to not have to ride herd on you.

Don't just sit and wait to be tasked to do something. Display some initiative. Pay attention, identify things that need doing, then do them. If you are unsure as to whether you *should* do them, just ask. Again, it's a golden opportunity to be seen in a favorable light by the boss. Bosses like industrious workers. The logic of this is inescapable.

Be on time. No matter how good the excuse for lateness, it's still an excuse, and excuses wear thin very quickly. Get your personal affairs in order so that they don't disrupt your job performance. Arrange for reliable transportation and, if needed, day care, and try to schedule medical, dental, and other appointments outside of work times.

As to the art of fitting in: We all want to be accepted by those with whom we associate every day. You can improve your chances by easing into your new role with moderation. Some helpful hints include:

- Listen more than you talk.

- Avoid profanity.

- Refrain from espousing radical concepts or taking controversial positions on social issues. (Oh, you can certainly have controversial opinions if you so choose, but it's not politically wise to risk alienating your coworkers—or your boss!—by hauling out the soap box and creating the impression that you're an extremist on a particular issue.)

- Be tasteful in your dress and grooming. Save the mini-skirt and halter-top for the club at night. Wear clothing that conceals the tattoo of the mating dogs. Wash the electric blue dye out of you rooster fan haircut, and comb it into a less spectacular style. Jewelry is a matter of taste, of course, but you can probably survive without your three nose rings during the work day. Bear in mind that most employers are conservative. While no one is trying to inhibit your right to individual expression, it is simply a fact that most bosses get very nervous about radical behavior from employees, and their nervousness usually translates to eroded confidence.

We realize that most of you will read these suggestions and wonder why we felt it necessary to include them. Simply stated, we've seen enough new workers to know that some people need the suggestions!

A former boss once said that he liked new employees who were "aggressively patient." That phrase pretty well sums up what we've said here. Be patient enough to fully adapt to your new surroundings, but aggressive enough to pounce on reasonable opportunities to display your abilities.

Good luck!

Federal Agency Listings

Before listing the federal agencies, we thought it would help those of you who have had no prior contact with the federal system to provide an explanation of the pay systems:

a. Most federal civilian positions are paid from a scale called the General Schedule. It contains pay grades ranging from GS-1 to GS-18. Once the pay grade is established, you are then assigned a pay level, or step. Pay steps are based primarily on longevity, but may also result from a meritorious pay increase for exceptional performance. The General Schedule pay table is published annually by the government. To figure out what you make, you simply find the row that shows your pay grade, and follow it across to the column for your step. Your annual pay is the amount shown where the row and column intersect. Look at Appendix E, the extract of the 1996 General Schedule. See? It's pretty self-explanatory. (NOTE: The 1997 General Schedule was not available for inclusion in this booklet.)

b. Military pay is based on a similar table, except that pay grades are determined by your status as an enlisted member or a commissioned officer. Enlisted soldiers get paid by their "E-_" grade, and officers by their "O-_" grade. It's the same process, though: row - column - bingo. See the extract 1997 military pay table at Appendix F.

c. Postal positions are slightly different, as well. The positions referred to in this booklet are paid from the Executive and Administrative Schedule (EAS). An extract of the 1997 EAS is at Appendix G.

Agency listings follow:

1. The Department of Agriculture
   14th Street and Independence Avenue, SW
   Washington, DC 20250
   Tele. (202) 447-2791

Within the Department of Agriculture, only the Office of the Inspector General offers criminal justice opportunities. Criminal Investigator positions are available in grades GS-5 thru -9. Call or write:

> Department of Agriculture
> Office of the Inspector General
> ATTN: Personnel Operations
> Washington, DC 20250
> Tele. (202) 447-6891

2. The Department of Commerce
14th Street and Constitution Avenue, NW
Washington, DC 20230
Tele. (202) 377-4948

Within the Department of Commerce, criminal justice positions are offered in the Office of the Inspector General (IG) and the Bureau of Export Administration (BEA). The position title in both agencies is Criminal Investigator. The grade range for the IG positions is GS-5 thru -7; the BEA range is GS-5 thru -9.

a. For information concerning an Office of the Inspector General position as a Criminal Investigator in grade range GS-5 thru -7, call or write one of the following locations:

Department of Commerce
Office of the Inspector General
ATTN: Personnel Office
14th Street and Constitution Avenue, NW, H7713
Washington, DC 20230
Tele. (202) 377-4948

Department of Commerce
Western Administrative Support Center
ATTN: Personnel Officer
7600 Sand Point Way, NE-BIN C15700
Seattle, WA 98115
Tele. (206) 526-6054

Department of Commerce
Mountain Administrative Support Center
ATTN: Personnel Officer
325 Broadway
Boulder, CO 80302
Tele. (303) 497-6305

b. For information concerning a Bureau of Export Administration position as a Criminal Investigator in grade range GS-5 thru -9, call or write:

Department of Commerce
Bureau of Export Administration
Office of Personnel Operations
14th Street and Constitution Avenue, NW, H1069
Washington, DC 20230
Tele. (202) 377-5138

3. The Department of Defense
The Pentagon
Washington, DC 20310
Tele. (202) 545-6700

Within the Department of Defense, criminal justice positions are offered by the military departments, the Defense Investigative Service, and the Defense Security Office. Depending on education and experience, military entry-level positions range from E-1 thru E-5 in the enlisted ranks to O-1 as a commissioned officer. The grade range for Defense Investigative Service Special Agent/Investigator positions is GS-5 thru -7. The Defense Police Officer grade range is GS-4 thru -6.

      a. For information concerning United States Air Force positions as a Security Police Officer or as a Special Agent in the Office of Special Investigations, call or write:

> Department of the Air Force
> The Pentagon
> Washington, DC 20330-1000
> Tele. (703) 545-6700

      b. For information concerning United States Army positions as a Military Police Officer or as a Special Agent in the Criminal Investigation Division, call or write:

> Department of the Army
> ATTN: TAPC-CPS-C
> 200 Stovall Street
> Alexandria, VA 22332-0320
> Tele. (202) 325-2130

      c. For information concerning United States Navy positions as a Shore Patrol Officer or as a Special Agent in the Naval Investigative Service, call or write:

> Department of the Navy
> Commander, Naval Investigative Service
> Washington, DC 20388-5000
> Tele. (202) 763-3780

      d. For information concerning a Defense Investigative Service position as a Special Agent (Investigator) in grade range GS-5 thru -7, call or write one of the following:

> Defense Investigative Service
> Personnel Operations Division
> 1900 Half Street, NW
> Washington, DC 20324-1700
> Tele: (202) 475-0575

Defense Investigative Service
Capital Region Personnel Office
Hoffman Building I
2461 Eisenhower Avenue
Alexandria, VA 22331-1000
Tele. (202) 325-9161

Defense Investigative Service
New England Region Personnel Office
495 Summer Street
Boston, MA 02210-2192
Tele. (617) 451-4904

Defense Investigative Service
Mid-Atlantic Region Personnel Office
1040 Kings Highway North
Cherry Hill, NJ 08034-1909
Tele. (609) 482-6500

Defense Investigative Service
Southeastern Region Personnel Office
2300 Lake Park Drive, Suite 250
Smyrna, GA 30080
Tele. (404) 432-0826

Defense Investigative Service
Midwestern Region Personnel Office
610 South Canal Street, Room 908
Chicago, IL 60607-4577
Tele. (312) 886-9062

Defense Investigative Service
Southwestern Region Personnel Office
210 North Tucker
St. Louis, MO 63188-1900
Tele. (314) 263-5345

Defense Investigative Service
Northwestern Region Personnel Office
Building 35, Room 114
Presidio of San Francisco, CA 94129-7700
Tele. (415) 561-5461

Defense Investigative Service
Pacific Region Personnel Office
3605 Long Beach Boulevard, Suite 405
Long Beach, CA 90807-4013
Tele. (213) 595-7183

e. For information concerning a Defense Security Office position as a Police Officer in grade range GS-4 thru -6, call or write:

Department of Defense
Personnel and Security
Washington Headquarters Services
Post Office Box 15249
Arlington, VA 22215
Tele. (202) 545-6700

4. The Department of Health and Human Services
200 Independence Avenue, SW
Washington, DC 20201
Tele. (202) 619-0257

Within the Department of Health and Human Services, only the Office of the Inspector General offers criminal justice opportunities. Criminal Investigator positions are available in grade range GS-5 thru -9. Call or write:

Department of Health and Human Services
Personnel Operations Group B
Office of the Assistant Secretary for Personnel Administration
330 Independence Avenue, SW
Washington, DC 20201
Tele. (202) 472-2516

5. The Department of Housing and Urban Development
451 Seventh Street, SW
Washington, DC 20410-1422
Tele. (202) 708-1422

Within the Department of Housing and Urban Development, criminal justice positions as a Criminal Investigator are offered in grade range GS-5 thru -9. Call or write:

Department of Housing and Urban Development
Chief, Staffing and Classification Branch
451 Seventh Street, SW, Room 2260
Washington, DC 20410-3100
Tele. (202) 755-5395

6. The Department of the Interior
18th and C Streets, NW
Washington, DC 20240
Tele. (202) 297-3171

Within the Department of the Interior, criminal justice positions are offered by the National Park Service, the U.S. Fish and Wildlife Service, the Bureau of Indian Affairs, and the Bureau of Land Management. The grade range for these positions is GS-3 thru -12.

a. For information concerning a National Park Service position as a Park Police Officer in grade range GS-3 thru -7, call or write:

> Department of the Interior
> National Park Service
> 18th and C Streets, NW
> Washington, DC 20013
> Tele. (202) 208-6843

b. For information concerning a U.S. Fish and Wildlife Service position as a Wildlife Special Agent in grade range GS-5 thru -12, call or write:

> Department of the Interior
> U.S. Fish and Wildlife Service
> 18th and C Streets, NW
> Washington, DC 20240
> Tele. (202) 208-5634

c. For information concerning a Bureau of Indian Affairs position as a Criminal Investigator in grade range GS-5 thru -9, call or write:

> Department of the Interior
> Bureau of Indian Affairs, Division of Personnel Management
> 1951 Constitution Avenue, NW
> Washington, DC 20240
> Tele. (202) 343-5547

d. For information concerning a Bureau of Land Management position as a Criminal Investigator in grade range GS-9 thru -13, call or write:

> Department of the Interior
> Bureau of Land Management, Division of Personnel
> 18th and C Streets, NW (MIB)
> Washington, DC 20240
> Tele. (202) 343-3193

7. The Department of Justice
Constitution Avenue and 10th Street, NW
Washington, DC 20530
Tele. (202) 514-2000

A wide range of criminal justice positions is offered by agencies within the Department of Justice. The grade range for these positions is GS-5 thru -12.

a. For information concerning specific opportunities in the Civil, Civil Rights, Criminal, Environment and Natural Resources, Tax, Antitrust, and Justice Management Divisions, call or write:

> Department of Justice
> Personnel Services
> Suite 6259, Main Building
> Constitution Avenue and 10th Street, NW
> Washington, DC 20530
> Tele. (202) 633-4615

b. For information concerning an Office of Justice Programs position as a Social Science Analyst in grade range GS-9 thru -12, call or write:

> Department of Justice
> Personnel Office, Office of Justice Programs
> 633 Indiana Avenue, NW
> Washington, DC 20531
> Tele. (202) 724-7725

c. For information concerning a Federal Bureau of Investigation position as a Special Agent in grade range GS-10 thru -13, call or write:

> Federal Bureau of Investigation
> 9th Street and Pennsylvania Avenue, NW
> Washington, DC 20535
> Tele. (202) 324-3000

(NOTE: Normally, Applicant Coordinators at FBI Field Offices serve as initial points of contact regarding employment with the Bureau. Write or call your local Field Office at the address and telephone number listed under "U.S. Government" in your telephone directory.)

d. For information concerning a Bureau of Prisons position as a Correctional Officer in grade GS-6, call or write one of the following:

Bureau of Prisons
Chief of Recruiting
Home Owners Loan Corporation Building, Room 400
320 First Street
Washington, DC 20534
Tele. (202) 724-3072

Bureau of Prisons
Personnel Officer, Northeast Region
2nd and Chestnut Streets
Philadelphia, PA 19106
Tele. (215) 597-6317

Bureau of Prisons
Personnel Officer, Mid-Atlantic Region
10010 Junction Drive, Suite 100N
Annapolis Junction, MD 20701
Tele. (301) 317-7000

Bureau of Prisons
Personnel Officer, Southeast Region
523 McDonough Boulevard, SE
Atlanta, GA 30315
Tele. (404) 624-5202

Bureau of Prisons
Personnel Officer, North Central Region
10920 Ambassador Drive
Kansas City, MO 64153
Tele. (816-891-7007

Bureau of Prisons
Personnel Officer, South Central Region
211 Cedar Springs Road
Dallas, TX 75219
Tele. (214) 767-9700

Bureau of Prisons
Personnel Officer, Western Region
7950 Dublin Boulevard
Dublin, CA 94568
Tele. (510) 803-4700

e. For information concerning a Drug Enforcement Administration position as a Special Agent in grade range GS-9 thru -12, call or write:

> Drug Enforcement Administration
> Office of Personnel
> 600-700 Army-Navy Drive
> Arlington, VA 22202
> Tele. (202) 307-4000

f. For information concerning an Immigration and Naturalization Service position as a Border Patrol Agent or Immigration Inspector (grade GS-5) or as a Special Agent (Criminal Investigator) (grade range GS-5 thru -7), call or write one of the following regional offices:

> Immigration and Naturalization Service
> Personnel Division
> 425 Eye Street, NW, Room 6032
> Washington, DC 20536
> Tele. (202) 786-3704

> Immigration and Naturalization Service
> Northern Region Personnel Division
> Federal Building, Fort Snelling
> Twin Cities, MN 55111
> Tele. (612) 725-3496

> Immigration and Naturalization Service
> Eastern Region Personnel Division
> Federal Building
> Burlington, VT 05401
> Tele. (802) 951-6255

> Immigration and Naturalization Service
> Southern Region Personnel Division
> Skyline Center, Building C
> 311 North Stemmons Freeway
> Dallas, TX 75207
> Tele. (214) 767-6070

> Immigration and Naturalization Service
> Western Region Personnel Division
> Terminal Island
> San Pedro, CA 90731
> Tele. (213) 514-6520

g. For information concerning Deputy U.S. Marshal positions in grade range GS-5 thru -7, call or write:

> U.S. Marshals Service
> 600 Army-Navy Drive
> Arlington, VA 22202
> Tele. (202) 307-9400

8. The Department of Labor
Frances Perkins Building
200 Constitution Avenue
Washington, DC 20210
Tele. (202) 523-8165

Within the Department of Labor, only the Office of the Inspector General offers criminal justice opportunities. Criminal Investigator positions are available in grade range GS-5 thru -7. Call or write:

> Department of Labor
> Office of Inspector General, Personnel Management Division
> Francis Perkins Building, Room S5021
> 200 Constitution Avenue
> Washington, DC 20210
> Tele. (202) 523-8165

9. The Department of State
2201 C Street, NW
Washington, DC 20520
Tele. (202) 647-4000

Within the Department of State, criminal justice opportunities are available in Special Agent and Security Officer positions. Call or write:

> Department of State
> Bureau of Diplomatic Security
> 2121 Virginia avenue, NW
> Washington, DC 20522-1003
> Tele. (703) 875-5481

10. The Department of Transportation
400 7th Street, SW
Washington, DC 20590
Tele. (202) 366-4000

Within the Department of Transportation, criminal justice positions are offered through the Office of the Inspector General and the U.S. Coast Guard.

a. For information concerning an Office of the Inspector General position as a Criminal Investigator in grade range GS-5 thru -9, call or write:

> Department of Transportation
> Office of the Inspector General, Room 7418
> Office of Personnel and Training, JP-30
> Washington, DC 20590
> Tele. (202) 366-2677

b. For information concerning U.S. Coast Guard positions as a Maritime Law Enforcement Officer, call or write:

> U.S. Coast Guard
> 2100 Second Street, SW
> Washington, DC
> Tele. (202) 267-1890

11. The Department of the Treasury
1500 Pennsylvania Avenue, NW
Washington, DC 20220
Tele. (202) 566-2000

Numerous agencies within the Department of the Treasury offer criminal justice opportunities. The grade range for these positions is GS- thru -12.

a. For information concerning a Departmental Offices position as a Criminal Investigator in grade range GS-5 thru -12, call or write:

> Department of the Treasury
> Office of Personnel Resources
> Departmental Offices, Employment Section, Room 1316
> 15th and Pennsylvania Avenue, NW
> Washington, DC 20220
> Tele. (202) 566-5411

b. For information concerning a Bureau of Alcohol, Tobacco, and Firearms position as a Special Agent or Inspector in grade range GS-5 thru -7, call or write:

Department of the Treasury
Bureau of Alcohol, Tobacco, and Firearms
Personnel Division, Room 1215
1200 Pennsylvania Avenue, NW
Washington, DC 20226
Tele. (202) 566-7321

c. For information concerning an Internal Revenue Service position as a Special Agent or Internal Security Inspector in grade range GS-5 thru -9, call or write:

Department of the Treasury
Internal Revenue Service
1111 Constitution Avenue, NW
Washington, DC 20224
Tele. (202) 566-5000

d. For information concerning U.S. Customs Service positions as an Inspector, Criminal Investigator, Treasury Enforcement Agent, Customs Investigator, Air Interdiction Officer, Intelligence Research Officer, or Special Agent, in grade range GS-5 thru -11, call or write:

U.S. Customs Service
Office of Human Resources
Servicewide Special Emphasis Program Coordinator
2120 L Street, Room 7402
Washington, DC 20229
Tele. (202) 634-5025

e. For information concerning a Bureau of Engraving and Printing position as a Police Officer or Security Specialist in grade range GS-5 thru -12, call or write:

Department of the Treasury
Bureau of Engraving and Printing
14th and C Streets, SW
Washington, DC 20228
Tele. (202) 447-0193

f. For information concerning a Federal Law Enforcement Center position as a Criminal Investigator Instructor, Training Instructor, or Law Enforcement Specialist Instructor in grade range GS-7 thru -11, call or write:

Department of the Treasury
Federal Law Enforcement Center
Glynco Facility
Glynco, GA 31524
Tele. (912) 267-2447

g. For information concerning a U.S. Secret Service position as a Special Agent or in the Uniformed Division in grade range GS-5 thru -7, call or write:

Department of the Treasury
U.S. Secret Service
1800 G Street, NW
Washington, DC 20223
Tele. (202)535-5708

12. Independent Agencies

a. The U.S. Capital Police
119 D Street, NE
Washington, DC 20510
Tele. (202) 224-9819

For information concerning a U.S. Capital Police position as a Police Officer, call or write the Personnel Department at the address and telephone number above.

b. Central Intelligence Agency
Washington, DC 20505
Tele. (202) 673-3916

For information concerning a Central Intelligence Agency position as an Agent in the Directorate of Operations or the Directorate of Intelligence, call or write:

Central Intelligence Agency
Personnel Representative (FCD)
P.O. Box 1925
Department S, Room 4N20
Washington, DC 20013
Tele. (703) 351-2141

c. The Equal Employment Opportunity Commission
1801 L. Street, NW
Washington, DC 20507
Tele. (202) 663-4900 or
      (800) 872-3362

For information concerning an Equal Employment Opportunity Commission position as an Investigator in grade range GS-5 thru -11, call or write:

Equal Employment Opportunity Commission
Personnel Office
1801 L Street, NW
Washington, DC 20507
Tele. (202) 63-4306

d. The Federal Emergency Management Agency
500 C Street, SW
Washington, DC 20472
Tele. (202) 646-4600

For information concerning a Federal Emergency Management Agency position as a Criminal Investigator in grade range GS-5 thru -9, call or write:

Federal Emergency Management Agency
Operations Division, Office of Personnel, Room 816
500 C Street, SW
Washington, DC 20472
Tele. (202) 646-4040

(NOTE: This agency's 24-hour Job Information Hotline number is [202] 646-4041.)

e. The General Services Administration
18th and F Streets, NW
Washington, DC 20405
Tele. (202) 708-5082

For information concerning a General Services Administration position as a Criminal Investigator or Federal Protective Service Officer in grade range GS-5 thru -7, call or write the appropriate Regional Personnel Office listed below:

General Services Administration
Regional Personnel Office, National Capital Region
Seventh and D Streets, SW
Washington, DC 20405
Tele. (202) 453-5300

General Services Administration
Regional Personnel Office, 2nd Region
26 Federal Plaza
New York, NY 10007
Tele. (212) 264-8295

General Services Administration
Regional Personnel Office, 3rd Region
Ninth and Market Streets
Philadelphia, PA 19107
Tele. (215) 597-0991

General Services Administration
Regional Personnel Office, 4th Region
1776 Peachtree Street, NW
Atlanta, GA 30309
Tele. (404) 242-3186

General Services Administration
Regional Personnel Office, 5th Region
230 South Dearborn Street
Chicago, IL 60604
Tele. (312) 353-5549

General Services Administration
Regional Personnel Office, 6th Region
1500 East Bannister Road
Kansas City, MO 64131
Tele. (816) 926-7401

General Services Administration
Regional Personnel Office, 7th Region
819 Taylor Street
Fort Worth, TX 76102
Tele. (817) 334-2361

General Services Administration
Regional Personnel Office, 9th Region
525 Market Street
San Francisco, CA 94105
Tele. (215) 454-9265

f. The Library of Congress
101 Independence Avenue, SE
Washington, DC 20540
Tele. (202) 707-5000

For information concerning a Library of Congress position as a Police Officer, call or write:

Library of Congress
Recruitment and Placement Division, Department E
101 Independence Avenue, SE, LM 107
Washington, DC 20540
Tele. (202) 707-5620

g. The Office of Personnel Management
1900 E Street, NW
Washington, DC 20415
Tele. (202) 606-1800

For information concerning an Office of Personnel Management position as an Investigator in grade range GS-5 thru -7, call or write:

Office of Personnel Management
Recruitment and Special Employment Programs branch
1900 E Street, NW, Room 1469
Washington, DC 20415
Tele. (202) 632-7484

h. The U.S. Government Printing Office
North Capitol and H Streets, NW
Washington, DC 20401
Tele. (202) 275-2051

For information concerning a Government Printing Office position as a Police Officer or Criminal Investigator in grade range GS-5 thru -7, call or write:

Government Printing Office
Chief, Employment Branch
Stop: PSE, North Capitol and H Streets, NW
Washington, DC 20401
Tele. (202) 275-1137

i. The U.S. Supreme Court
One First Street, NE
Washington, DC 20453
Tele. (202) 479-3404

For information concerning a U.S. Supreme Court position as a Police Officer, call or write the Personnel Officer at the address and telephone number listed above.

j. The U.S. Postal Service
475 L'Enfant Plaza West, SW
Washington, DC 20260
Tele. (202) 268-2000

For information concerning a U.S. Postal Service position as a Postal Inspector in grade range EAS-17 thru -23, call or write:

U.S. Postal Service
General Manager, Headquarters Personnel Division
475 L'Enfant Plaza West, SW
Washington, DC 20260
Tele. (202) 268-3646

Samples From the Web

1. CECIL GREEK'S *CRIMINAL JUSTICE LINKS*

Cecil Greek's Criminal Justice Page   http://www.fsu.edu/~crimdo/cj.html#police

Alcatraz

Criminal Justice Resources on the Web

Last Updated 10-1-96

We're Linked!!

 Selected Site of the Week by Law Enforcement Links

U.S. News and World Report on the War on Crime

Order the Latest Criminal Justice Books

🔵 Federal Criminal Justice Agencies

🔵 International Criminal Justice Sources

🔵 Criminal Justice Information

 Crime and Crime Prevention Pages: New Subheadings

🔵 Juvenile Delinquency

🔵 Drug and Alcohol Information

🔵 Police Agencies and Resources

🔵 The Courts: Due Process and Civil Liberties

🔵 Obscenity, Censorship & The Communications Decency Act

🔵 Prisons and the Death Penalty

🔵 Searchable Law Databases

🔵 Other Law Sites on the Web

🔵 Criminal Justice Education: Includes Forensics

🔵 On-line Criminal Justice Discussion Groups and E-Journals

🔵 Criminal Justice Images and Illustrations

🔵 Criminal Justice in the Media

🔵 Criminal Justice Photos

🔵 O.J.Trial Photos--From Reuter's News Service (copyrighted images)

2. CECILE GREEK'S *LAW ENFORCEMENT AGENCIES ON THE WEB*

Last updated 9-30-96

NEW Order the Latest <u>Criminal Justice</u> **Books**

● <u>College And University Police Departments</u>

● <u>State Law Enforcement Agencies</u>

● <u>Municipal Police Departments and County Sheriffs</u>

● <u>Military Police Departments</u>

● <u>Police Agencies Outside the United States</u>

● <u>Miscellaneous Law Enforcement Programs</u>

College and University Police Departments

● <u>University of South Florida at St. Petersburg Campus Police</u>

● <u>University of Alberta Campus Security Services</u>

● <u>Baylor University Dept. of Public Safety</u>

● <u>Brigham Young University Gopher</u>

EMPLOYMENT OPPORTUNITIES   http://www.sirinet.net/~lawtonpd/employ.htm

Updated 6-21-96

EMPLOYMENT OPPORTUNITIES AT THE LAWTON POLICE DEPARTMENT

"Striving for Excellence . . ."

The Lawton Police Department, an equal opportunity employer, is a growing law enforcement agency that provides a variety of specialization fields for those wishing to become police officers. The Lawton Police Department has five divisions: Headquarters, Uniform, Criminal Investigation, Technical Services, and Training. Specialized sections of these divisions include special operations (vice and narcotics), detectives, traffic, patrol, lake patrol, bicycle patrol, D.A.R.E., and crime prevention. Generally, all new officers are assigned to uniform patrol duties for the first three years of their employment. After that, requests to transfer to other duties will be considered as vacancies are identified. To become a Lawton Police Officer, an applicant must follow and meet the requirements outlined below.

- MINIMUM ELIGIBILITY REQUIREMENTS
- TESTING
- TRAINING
- SALARY AND COMPENSATION
- BENEFITS
- UNIFORMS AND EQUIPMENT
- PROMOTIONAL ADVANCEMENT OPPORTUNITIES
- APPLICATION PROCEDURES

MINIMUM ELIGIBILITY REQUIREMENTS

- Must be a United States citizen
- Must have a high school diploma or GED
- Must be at least 21 years of age
- Applicants having prior military experience must have an honorable discharge or an uncharacterized discharge which allows for re-enlistment into the military service (Note: Prior military experience is not a requirement.)
- Must possess an unrestricted Oklahoma driver's license (except for corrective lenses) or a comparable driver's license from another state of the United States
- Must agree to abide by the City of Lawton's personnel rules, Administrative

Directives, and the Lawton Police Department Operations Manual (which includes rules, regulations, policies, and procedures)

- Must not be the subject of or under any criminal investigation (civilian or military) during the application process for conduct which could possibly result in:
  - Probation or parole
  - Fines
  - Jail Time
  - Prison Time
- Must have no felony convictions
- Must have no misdemeanor convictions within the last 3 years
- Must not have more than 2 misdemeanor convictions within the last 10 years or since your 18th birthday
- Must not be living with anyone who:
  - Has been convicted of 2 or more felonies
  - Has been convicted of a felony within the last 5 years
  - Has been convicted of more than 2 misdemeanors within the last 2 years
  - Is currently a fugitive from justice (Note: A fugitive from justice is defined as any person who has committed any felony or misdemeanor for which they are subject to arrest and prosecution at the time of application.)
- Must not be on probation for any crime at the time of the application
- Must not admit nor have been convicted of:
  - Sexual assault (of any kind)
  - Public lewdness
  - Indecent exposure
- Must not have been arrested for use or sale of illegal drugs. Applicants who have used illegal drugs may not be automatically excluded from consideration for employment. Determining factors for further consideration is based on frequency of use, last date used, and type of drug used.
- Must not have been arrested for D.U.I., D.W.I., or A.P.C. within the last five (5) years.
- Must not have been convicted of 4 or more traffic violations within the last ten (10) years or since your 18th birthday and must not have any within the last six (6) months.
- Must not have been convicted of driving with a suspended or revoked license within the last five (5) years.
- Must be able to pass an extensive background investigation relating to driving records, criminal records, and financial responsibility records.
- Must not make any false statement concerning a "material fact" in the application process. A "material fact" is any fact concerning the applicant, which, if brought to the attention of the Police Department, would result in the applicant's rejection from the selection process. Grounds for rejection includes falsification of the application by omission or deception in the areas of:
  - Employment information

- ☐ Criminal activity (misdemeanor and/or felony)
- ☐ Theft from employer(s)
- ☐ Illegal drug usage
- ☐ Driving history
- ☐ Military history

☐ Undesirable conduct in the area of integrity, discipline, commitment, or reliability may cause an applicant to be disqualified.

☐ Must have a stable employment record. Instability may include the inability to maintain steady employment as well as gross abuse of standards, incompetency, or aberrant behavior during a single employment.

☐ Must not have a credit history which could result in criminal prosecution (i.e. failure to pay child support) or conduct which appears intended to defraud or harm just creditors.

TESTING

Applicants are required to complete and pass each of the following to enter the police academy:

☐ **Physical Ability** - This is a timed event in which the applicant must listen and follow exact directions, run, climb a 6-foot fence, low crawl, climb through a window, identify a suspect based on a given description, and drag a dummy that weighs approximately 150 pounds for a prescribed distance.

☐ **Written Examination** - The examination is based on a study guide given to the applicants who successfully complete the physical ability.

☐ **Oral Interviews** - A total of two oral interviews are conducted. The first interview is conducted by a panel of police officers and civilians. The second interview occurs during the final stages of the process and is conducted by the Chief of Police and other ranking members of the Department.

Extensive Background Investigation - The background investigation includes, but is not limited to, previous employment, traffic and criminal checks, education, financial responsibility, and character references as previously outlined.

Psychological Examination - The psychological examination includes completion of the MMPI and CPI tests including interpretation by a licensed practitioner trained to evaluate results of both tests.

Extensive Physical Examination - Physical examinations include a complete medical examination and evaluation.

Drug Screening - Complete blood testing is performed to check for any illegal substance.

Polygraph - A polygraph test is administrated to the candidate to verify the statements made on their application.

TRAINING

The Lawton Police Academy includes approximately 324 hours of instruction in a Basic Police Academy conducted by the Oklahoma Council on Law Enforcement, Education, and Training in Oklahoma City. During this training, recruits receive a salary and are provided meals and lodging. Successful completion of the basic academy is mandatory for continued employment. Training includes showing a proficiency (through written examinations and/or demonstration) in the areas of Oklahoma criminal laws, First Aid/CPR, Firearms, Emergency Driving, human relations, communications, etc.

Following the Basic Academy, 160 hours of specialized local training is conducted by the Lawton Police Department. Upon graduation from both training phases, recruits are sworn in and begin a 16 week Field Officer Training Program where they receive on-the-job training from an experienced patrol officer.

SALARY AND COMPENSATION

1. **WAGES** -

   The Lawton Police Department recruits start earning a salary from the first day of employment (including training). Police Officers are paid biweekly and can look forward to a series of step increases based on merit. Beginning base pay (not including any other fringe benefits) is $10.96 per hour for the first 6 months. A 5% merit increase raises the salary to $11.51 per hour for the next 6 months, and another 5% merit increase raises the salary to $12.09 per hour after the first year. Employees may receive 5% merit raises on the anniversary date of their hiring for each of the next 4 years.

2. **LONGEVITY PAY** -

   Employees begin accruing longevity pay credits upon completion of 48 months of continuous service with the City. Although paid once a year, an officer's longevity pay credits are equal to 4.4571 times the officer's total number of years of continuous service with the City.

3. **ACTING CLASSIFICATION PAY** -

   Employees authorized to perform the duties of a position classification one level above their own position classification are paid an additional 10% if the duties are performed more than 24 hours in a 40 hour work period.

4. **DETECTIVE PAY** -

   Employees working in detectives/investigators assignments receive 5% additional pay.

5. **MASTER OFFICER PAY** -

   Employees may also receive 5% proficiency pay and be designated a Master

Officer after 4 years of employment with the Lawton Police Department.

6. **NIGHT WORK PAY DIFFERENTIAL** -

Officers who work at least 50% of their scheduled day's work between the hours of 5:00 p.m. and 8:00 a.m. receive 5% for Night Work Pay Differential.

BENEFITS

The benefits that await those who become Lawton Police Officers are:

1. Up to 80 hours of extra pay for **Holidays** each year
2. 80 hours of **Paid Vacation** following completion of the first year's employment. The amount of paid vacation times increases periodically until maxing out at 160 hours after 16 years of employment
3. **Life Insurance**
4. 96 hours of **Paid Sick Leave** each year; unused sick leave can accumulate to 576 hours after which time you will be paid for any sick leave that exceeds 576 hours at regular salary rates
5. 24 hours of **Paid Bereavement Leave** for loss of family members as identified in the labor agreement
6. Up to 20 days **Paid Military Leave** for members of a military Reserve unit or the National Guard
7. **Retirement Program** with the Oklahoma Police Officer's Pension System which allows officers to retire at 50% after 20 years of service or 75% after 30 years of service (Vested Retirement after 10 years at a reduced rate)
8. Time and a half in pay or compensated time off for **Overtime**
9. **Paid Employment Health Plan** (100% for employees plus partial for family members when employees pay the balance for the family plan)
10. 90% **Educational Reimbursement** for books and tuition for successful completion of approved courses

UNIFORMS AND EQUIPMENT

The City of Lawton provides all duty-required:
Uniforms
Leather Goods
Footwear
Coats
Hats
Weapons

Vehicles

PROMOTIONAL ADVANCEMENT OPPORTUNITIES

Officers become eligible for promotion through time in service/grade, various written and oral examinations, and university/college credit hours.

APPLICATION PROCEDURE

To begin the application procedure, contact the Personnel Office at the address listed below. Your name will be placed on a contact list until the next testing cycle is scheduled. Once the testing cycle is scheduled, you will be contacted and provided with further instructions.

A personally challenging and exciting career awaits those who have what it takes to be a Lawton Police Officer.

For more information contact:
City of Lawton
Personnel Department
Owens Multi-Purpose Center
1405 SW 11th Street
Lawton, Oklahoma 73501
(405) 581-3392

Back to the Lawton Police Department Main Page

4. *DEA SPECIAL AGENT*

To view this document in a non-graphics mode, please click here

● Be a part of the solution...
   ● Be a part of our future...

Background

Are You Up to the Challenge?

Qualifications

Conditions of Employment

Salary & Benefits

Recruiter Locations

44

5. *JEFFERSON COUNTY, COLORADO, SHERIFF'S DEPARTMENT*

...JCSD IS NOT Hiring At This Time....

Jefferson County Sheriff's Department Information

At The Present Time, JCSD IS NOT Hiring

For additional information, contact the Jefferson County S.O. Recruiting and Training unit at 303/271-5350. Or to be placed on the S.O.'s mailing list at application time, call 303/271-5350 and tell the secretary what job you are interested in. She should place your name on a mailing list.

Also, feel free to call the county's 24 hour Job Line at 303/271-8401

Applicants for the position of Deputy Sheriff must meet the following minimun requirements:

- ☐ Be 21 years of age.
- ☐ Be Colorado P.O.S.T. certified/certifiable.
- ☐ Possess a valid Colorado Drivers License.
- ☐ Although not required, 60 credits from an accredited college is preferred.

Main Jobs Page

This Page Accessed
9 1 Times
Since 091396.

Page layout and design: Copyright Glenn B Howell, 1996

6. *FLORIDA STATE ATTORNEY GENERAL BOB BUTTERWORTH*

SPECIAL ALERT: Alleged price-gouging associated with Tropical Storm Josephine may be reported to our hotline at 1-800-329-6969. Click here for details.

News Releases	Citizen Safety	Legal Opinions
Consumer Investigations	Consumer Information	Lemon Law
Crime Victims Services	Government in the Sunshine	Job Opportunities
Criminal Justice	Statewide Prosecution	Other AGs
Florida's Attorney General	AG Services & Units	Phone Numbers, Addresses & Maps

Text-Based Browsers

Rated by Point Survey as among the top 5 percent of sites on the Web
Awarded a four-star rating by Magellan

7. *ILLINOIS CRIMINAL JUSTICE INFORMATION AUTHORITY*

If you have any questions about this WWW site, contact webmaster@icjia.org
© 1995 Illinois Criminal Justice Information Authority. All rights reserved

This page has been accessed   times since 7/26/96.

Last Updated: 5/3/96

If you have any questions about this WWW site, contact webmaster@icjia.org
© 1995 Illinois Criminal Justice Information Authority. All rights reserved

This site uses extensions that can *only* be viewed using Netscape 2.0  or Microsoft

Explorer 3.0

47

Illinois Criminal Justice Information Authority
Employment Opportunities

● Client/Server Software Developer - *added 8/5/96*

● Database/Internet System Designer - *added 8/5/96*

● Technical Support Specialist - *added 9/23/96*

● Victim Service Specialist - *added 8/18/96*

Client/Server Software Developer - *Information Systems Unit*

Help fight crime! Join a small team environment where you can stand out converting and enhancing our premiere law enforcement systems using Client/Server and wireless technology. We seek motivated individuals with a successful track record developing quality, engineered software to be involved in all development phases. Any combination of skills w/C, C++, VB, OOP, HP MPE and/or Windows component building exp a plus. Competitive salary and excellent benefits. Knowledge/exp equiv. to 4 yr. Computer Science degree required.

Resumes to:
Illinois Criminal Justice Information Authority
120 S. Riverside Plaza Suite 1016
Chicago, IL 60606
ATTN: Jan Oncken
FAX: 312-793-8422
e-mail: Jan Oncken

Added 8/5/96

Database/Internet System Designer - *Information Systems Unit*

Seeking individual to design, implement and support program site databases and internet and/or modem-based linkages. Also required recommending all hardware and software for the system and it's sites. Knowledge/exp. equiv. to 4 yr. degree in Computer Science and 3 yrs. experience. in Database Design. Also experience with DOS, Windows 3.1 and Windows 95, Microsoft Access, HTML, Novell,

Quattro Pro and WordPerfect. Contractural position. Monetary compensation in lieu of insurance benefits.

Resume and salary req to:
Illinois Criminal Justice Information Authority
120 S. Riverside Plaza Suite 1016
Chicago, IL 60606
ATTN: Jan Oncken
FAX: 312-793-8422
e-mail: Jan Oncken

Added 8/5/96

Technical Support Specialist - *Information Systems Unit*

Extensive customer contact, requires knowledge in setup, configuration, troubleshooting & user support activities in large scale Netware, Windows NT, TCP/IP LAN and WAN environments. All positions require minimum of a Bachelors degree in Computer Science or equivalent work experience. Competitive salary, excellent benefits.

Resumes to:
Illinois Criminal Justice Information Authority
120 S. Riverside Plaza Suite 1016
Chicago, IL 60606
ATTN: Jan Oncken
FAX: 312-793-8422
e-mail: Jan Oncken

Published 09/22/96 - Chicago Tribune

Victim Service Specialist - *Federal & State Grants Unit*

State agency seeks individual to perform functions relating to the planning, develop, implementation, & monitoring of programs for the direct service delivery to victims of violent crimes. Participates in the compiling of statistical & informational data for use in reports & presentations. Requires degree in field of study related to victim services or equivalent experience. Experience in planning & delivery of crime victim services helpful. Experience with WordPerfect 6.1 & Quattro Pro for Windows. Valid drivers license with some travel requirements. Salary $27K-$38K. Contractual position. Monetary compensation in lieu of employer paid insurance benefits.

Resumes to:
Illinois Criminal Justice Information Authority
120 S. Riverside Plaza Suite 1016
Chicago, IL 60606
ATTN: Jan Oncken
FAX: 312-793-8422
e-mail: Jan Oncken

Added 8/18/96

Helpful Hints

for

Completing and Submitting

Federal Employment

Application Forms (SF-171/OF-612)

Application for Federal Employment (Standard Form 171):

To put it mildly, the process of completing and submitting your Application for Federal Employment (which we will hereafter refer to as the SF-171) can be the most intimidating, frustrating, disheartening, mind-boggling experience you've ever been through. Why? Because in order to get the SF-171 into the system, you have to venture deep into the world of—GOVERNMENT BUREAUCRACY!

Since it just can't be avoided, we thought you could use some helpful guidance and an example of a well done SF-171. We offer some ideas to help you prepare a better application, to get it into the system with a better chance of being considered, and to reduce the hassle it can sometimes become. We also offer some do's and don'ts.

These suggestions are not presented in any particular sequence relative to the application process. We just wrote them down as they came to mind. It might be beneficial to read through the whole list before you begin the actual process of completing your application, because we might show you a trick or two to save a little work (and a lot of "do-overs"!).

Appendix I provides a completed SF-171. Let's take a tour of it, and we'll point out some important things to keep in mind.

The first thing you should note is the clean, professional appearance. This piece of paper is representing you to those who are considering you for employment. If it looks sloppy or incomplete, it will speak volumes about your work habits to those who will read it. Their impression of you won't be very good, either. (*"If this person does sloppy work on forms that are for their _own_ good, how much worse will they do on work_I_want them to do."*)

Which leads us to SUGGESTION NO. 1: *Make your SF-171 nice to look at and easy to follow.*

    a. Make sure entries in each block are *in the block,* not crowding over the lines, and that the reader can clearly identify each response.

    b. Clearly indicate the scope of supervisory responsibility for each job in terms of manpower, property, and financial resources for which you were responsible.

    c. Vertically align repetitive data in sequential blocks.

    d. List accomplishments that reflect favorable organizational impact resulting from your performance.

    e. If you have military experience, civilianize military terminology. (For example, use the commonly understood term "General Manager" to replace the military-unique term "Company Commander," which may confuse a civilian reviewer who is unfamiliar with military organizations.)

    f. DO NOT fill this form out by hand.

And here's SUGGESTION NO. 2: *Consider hiring professionals to do your form.* Most resume services also do SF-171s. Check your yellow pages. It is likely that the people who prepare these things for a living will be just a tad better at doing them than the rest of us. They understand the importance of a professional image, and have the skill and equipment to prepare the forms correctly. But watch out! Ask around about the place you're considering. Sometimes the prices can be out of sight, and the quality can be less than desirable. Reputation says it all in this business. If an outfit has lots of satisfied customers, they're a pretty safe bet. But if people bad-mouth them, find someone else.

See block 13, the one that asks *where* you'd be willing to work? SUGGESTION NO. 3: Say you'll accept a job anywhere. If you don't want to take an offered job, you can always decline, but if you put a limit on the jobs they can offer, you reduce the opportunity to <u>get</u> an offer.

Watch out for block 23 at the top of page 2, and block 37 at the top of page 4. Remember to select either 'yes' or 'no' in both blocks. If you leave them blank, your application may be returned to you for a response to that question, which would cause you to miss the application deadline date. It is also possible that the application may simply be returned to you without action.

That ushers in SUGGESTION NO. 4:

DO NOT LEAVE <u>ANY</u> BLOCK ON THE SF-171 BLANK!

Remember what we said about government bureaucracy? Well, the reason it continues to exist is that government has a high concentration of *bureaucrats*. They often find it convenient to identify the very first possible reason to eliminate your application from the pile of work they have to do. A blank space—<u>ANY</u> blank space—is a *perfect* reason. **DO NOT GIVE IT TO THEM!** No matter what the block asks for, give 'em an answer, even if it's just "N/A." Make the reader know that you did, in fact, look at that particular block, and that you made a conscious decision to not answer the question it asks. If you don't, the reader (meaning "the one who is reading your application to see if you merit any further consideration for the job for which you applied") may decide to remove your application from consideration because of the unanswered question. **You'll never get hired if you never get past the initial screening.**

Now look at block 24-B on page 2. Notice that the cited experience is volunteer work. Yes, you can list experience you obtain in this manner, and it is often very advantageous to do so. The same thing holds true for the public speaking and computer skills entries in block 32. You can list any skill, no matter how you acquired it, as long as you can substantiate your claimed level of competence.

SUGGESTION NO. 5: Whether you decide to do your own SF-171 or have it done for you, *collect everything you'll need to complete the form.*

a. If you're a veteran, get copies of <u>all</u> your DD-214s (Reports of Separation or Discharge from Active Service). They contain essential data you will need to accurately complete various blocks on the SF-171.

b. If you are eligible for the 10-point veteran preference, complete a SF-15 (Application for 10-Point Veteran Preference) and get copies of the documents substantiating your entitlement to the preference.

c. Gather all past work descriptions, performance evaluation reports received from past employers, and any other documents that can assist you in remembering details of previous jobs you've held. Prospective employers do not—repeat, **DO NOT**—want to read endless descriptions of all the minor little tasks you did in each job. But they **DO** want to read all about what you did to improve productivity, save money, cause growth in your department, effectively supervise your subordinates, or otherwise contribute in a positive way to the success of your former employer's business. Performance appraisals, etc., can jog your memory, but whatever you do, <u>don't embellish!</u> Present facts and figures that your past employer can and will verify if the new guy calls for a reference.

d. Get copies of your high school diploma, GED certificate, college transcripts and diplomas, trade or technical school certificates or diplomas (including military training courses), and any other documents that substantiate your successful completion of any schools or formal courses.

e. Get documents verifying completion of any apprenticeship program or formal on-the-job training program.

f. If you hold any special licenses or qualifications, get whatever documents you have to substantiate the license or qualification. If the license is renewable or is contingent on some other qualification (such as passing a flight physical to maintain currency as a pilot), ensure you have documents validating the latest update.

g. If you have a language skill in addition to English, including sign language, obtain documents that verify your reading and speaking comprehension levels. If you have to pay to be professionally tested, we recommend you do so. Your language skill gives you a very real edge in a highly competitive job market, but only if it is adequately documented. And be prepared to take your entire interview in the language in which you claim proficiency.

h. Decide on three people you intend to use as references, then get their correct names, (including the correct spellings), the titles they prefer (*Doctor* Jones may be offended by being addressed as *Mister* Jones), and their correct addresses and telephone numbers. It is usually a smart idea to contact each of them in advance. They will appreciate the courtesy of being asked for a reference and being forewarned that they might be called. Your call also gives you the opportunity to find out whether they would prefer listing their home or work address and telephone number in the "References" block of the SF-171.

i. If you have been convicted of any crime(s), civilian or military, or are currently pending charges, gather all the information pertaining to the incident(s). The fact that you have a criminal record will not prevent your being hired, but it is essential that you be up front and accurate when providing details. If the prospective employer thinks you are trying to conceal anything, you will have no chance. You can eliminate concerns by having the information regarding the offense readily available to answer questions or complete required forms.

SUGGESTION NO. 6: *If your work history includes managerial experience, tell them how well you managed*, not how you did the work yourself!. Let's say that you ran a small manufacturing plant with, oh, 100 employees working three shifts. Do not put down on that form that you supervised 100 employees on three shifts! If you do, you'll be saying that you never slept and that you performed a managerial impossibility on a daily basis, because no one can work around the clock every day, or supervise 100 people effectively.

The best way to say it—the way that tells your prospective employer that you are an effective and efficient manager (which is probably what you are asking to be hired as!)—is something like this: "Supervised eight subordinate managers guiding the efforts of 92 skilled technicians on three manufacturing shifts." This statement tells the reader that you understand span of control; that you have confidence in your ability to train your subordinates to do things right even when you're not there; and that you understand your role and will do the job for which you are being paid.

SUGGESTION NO. 7: *Do not spend your time and money hand-carrying your SF-171 to the servicing Federal Office of Personnel Management or the personnel department of the agency to which you are applying.* Some people believe it gives them an edge to personally deliver an application. Maybe it does in some settings, but it has no impact when you are dealing with government agencies. If it is convenient to do so, by all means, deliver it. But in almost all cases, your application will be accepted by a low-level clerk who will not be at all impressed by your effort or how spiffy you look in your new suit. Mail it, or send it via a private delivery firm such as Federal Express. (See next suggestion.)

SUGGESTION NO. 8: *Mail your SF-171 via Certified Mail and get a return receipt, or send it via Federal Express.* Why? Because bureaucracies tend to swallow things whole, and it is easy for your application to disappear without a trace. If you have cause to believe you were unjustly denied an opportunity to compete for a position for which you are fully qualified, you can seek administrative or legal relief. First, however, you have to prove they had your application to begin with! If you deliver it yourself, no one will sign for it. But if you send it as suggested, someone MUST sign for it. Voila—proof! (Neat, huh?)

SUGGESTION NO. 9: *Do not leave gaps in documentation of employment dates.* Suppose you worked at one place from June of 1988 until September of 1990, then got laid off. Let's say you were out of work for three months, then hired into your new job in January, 1991. List the period from September 1990 until January 1991 as "Unemployed," and explain in the "Description of Work" block that you were laid off because of company downsizing or whatever. Your potential new boss understands that, and assigns no stigma to it. But not accounting for the gap in time causes the prospective employer to have doubts. You want to be viewed in a positive light; doubt isn't positive.

SUGGESTION NO. 10: *Do not give up!* T-E-N-A-C-I-T-Y is the name of this game. Don't get discouraged because you send in lots of applications but get no calls. Be patient. Try to understand that there's not a lot of "hurry" in the hiring end of the government. So relax, and don't get upset if the vacancy for which you applied is filled before they get to you. One of the most remarkable features of the government is its awesome size. It does not have *one* of anything, so it will undoubtedly come up with another vacancy in your field before too long. Just hang in there.

Optional Application for Federal Employment (Optional Form 171):

The OF-612 is a cut-down version of the SF-171. Among other changes, it eliminates questions regarding such factors as gender, age, and criminal records, and the requirement to list specific dates of military service (if any) or specific subjects taken in achieving undergraduate or graduate degrees. It is much easier to complete, but keep in mind each of the suggestions listed above. In particular:

a. Keep it neat and professional looking.

b. Don't leave any blank blocks!

c. Provide concise, accurate job descriptions.

d. Organize your supporting material so that you can produce documentary evidence of claimed experience, education, and special qualifications (licenses, languages, etc.) in the event you are called for an interview.

e. Get your references squared away just as you would for the SF-171. (See paragraph h, above.)

f. Use certified mail, FEDEX, or some other means of getting it delivered and obtaining a receipt to show they got it.

g. Be patient, and don't give up.

Okay, that's it for the helpful hints. At the end of the booklet, we have included blank copies of all pages of the SF-171 and its partner form, the SF-171A (Continuation Sheet for SF-171), and the OF-612. If you are unable to the forms elsewhere, you can always duplicate these.

It may appear that your pursuit of federal employment is too big a headache, but don't let these forms intimidate you. Plenty of folks have gotten them filled out correctly and were hired; you can be, too. Follow the hints in this appendix and keep a positive attitude. Hopefully, your job search will be a short one.

Sample Resumes

1. FULL RESUME

RESUME

WALTER R. SCHMEDLAPP   voice: (810) 474-6240
26127 Kiltartan   fax: (810) 927-5876
Farmington Hills, Michigan 48084   e-mail: schmed@aol.com

EDUCATION

Master of Science, Criminal Justice, June 1992. Michigan State University, East Lansing, Michigan.

Bachelor of Science, Psychology, May 1986. Campbell University, Buie's Creek, North Carolina.

EXPERIENCE

SECTION MANAGER, Oakland County Probation Department, Pontiac, Michigan. February 1994-Present.

Supervise nine case officers and two clerical workers in a probation management section overseeing an average caseload of 208 probationers per case officer.

Manage administrative processes including files/records management; internal and external distribution services; blank forms supply; word processing operations; and preparation of all correspondence.

Perform aspects of human resources operations such as interviewing, hiring/firing, policy development, training, employee relations, safety, performance evaluation and counseling, implementation and administration of federally mandated Affirmative Action and Equal Employment Opportunity programs, and compliance with applicable state and federal employment requirements.

Responsible for the serviceability, maintenance, accountability and utilization of facilities and equipment valued in excess of $130,000.

Manage a $350,000 annual budget. Prepare budget projections for all section activities. Submit and defend the annual budget input.

LECTURER (Part-time), Oakland Community College, Farmington Hills, Michigan. September 1994-Present.

Instruct classes of up to thirty students of all grade levels in a variety of introductory criminal justice courses, including Introduction to Criminal Justice, Introduction to Law Enforcement, Organized Crime, Legal Aspects of Criminal Justice, Police-Community Relations, Police Organization and

Administration, Criminal Justice Management and Operations, Criminal Justice Issues, the American Criminal Court System, Judicial Process, Juvenile Delinquency, Probation and Parole, Introduction to Corrections, and Community-Based Corrections. Supervise students completing internship assignments with various local criminal justice agencies. Advise students seeking guidance in pursuit of academic, occupational, and personal goals.

CASE OFFICER, Oakland County Probation Department, Pontiac, Michigan. August 1987-February 1994.

Managed an average caseload of 200+ felony and misdemeanor offenders. Conducted personal interviews of probationers to ascertain progress toward rehabilitation. Provided advice and counsel as needed on such matters as employment, control of drug and alcohol use, resolution of family and personal conflicts, financial responsibility, and avoidance of potential problem behavior. Identified non-responsive probationers and formulated recommendations for program modification appropriate to the degree of nonperformance.

SOLDIER, U.S. Army, July 1983-July 1987.

Held sequential Military Police assignments of increasing responsibility, including:

PATROL SERGEANT, Fort Bragg, North Carolina, November 1986-July 1987.

Supervised six subordinate managers guiding the patrol activities of 48 patrol officers on a major military installation with a combined military and civilian population of 112,000.

Prepared all shift schedules to ensure adequate coverage of assigned patrol areas and special police support commitments.

Developed and conducted all training of assigned personnel in general soldiering and unique police technical subject areas.

DESK SERGEANT, Republic of Korea, November 1985-November 1986.

Supervised a four-member police dispatch and booking operations staff on a major military encampment with a combined U.S. and foreign national military and civilian population of 23,000.

Maintained records of all calls for police assistance and reports of patrol activities. Assigned available response units as needed. Created and maintained booking records on all arrested suspects. Served as liaison to local foreign national police units on incidents involving U.S. and foreign national protagonists.

Developed and conducted all training of assigned personnel in general soldiering and unique police technical subject areas.

ASSISTANT OPERATIONS SERGEANT, Republic of Korea, January-November 1985.

Responsible for planning and scheduling of training and contingency operations for a 290-member military police organization on a major military encampment with a combined U.S. and foreign national military and civilian population of 23,000.

Coordinated logistical and transportation support for all training and contingency operations.

Maintained essential records documenting individual and unit accomplishment of mandatory training requirements such as firearms, swimming, lifesaving, driver safety, alcohol and drug abuse, and such specialized subject matter as may be dictated by higher headquarters.

PATROL OFFICER, Fort Carson, Colorado, December 1983-January 1985.

Conducted routine and special police patrol activities on a major military installation with a combined military and civilian population of 84,000.

COMMUNITY SERVICE

Board Member, Oakland County Jaycees. September 1988-Present.

Member, Oakland County Big Brothers, September 1988-Present.

President, Kimberly Subdivision Neighborhood Watch, April 1989-April 1991.

2. ABBREVIATED RESUME

RESUME

WALTER R. SCHMEDLAPP
26127 Kiltartan
Farmington Hills, Michigan 48084

voice: **(810) 474-6240**
fax: **(810) 927-5876**
e-mail: **schmed@aol.com**

EDUCATION

Master of Science, Criminal Justice, June 1992. Michigan State University, East Lansing, Michigan.

Bachelor of Science, Psychology, May 1986. Campbell University, Buie's Creek, North Carolina.

EXPERIENCE

SECTION MANAGER, Oakland County Probation Department, Pontiac, Michigan. February 1994-Present.

Supervise daily operations of a probation section staffed with nine case officers and two clerical workers. Oversee management of an average caseload of 208 probationers per case officer.

LECTURER (Part-time), Oakland Community College, Farmington Hills, Michigan. September 1994-Present.

Instruct classes of up to thirty students of all grade levels in a variety of introductory criminal justice courses.

CASE OFFICER, Oakland County Probation Department, Pontiac, Michigan. August 1987-February 1994.

Conducted individual case management for an average caseload of 200+ felony and misdemeanor offenders

SOLDIER, U.S. Army, July 1983-July 1987.

Held sequential Military Police assignments of increasing responsibility, including Patrol Officer, Patrol Team Leader, Assistant Operations Sergeant, Desk Sergeant, and Patrol Sergeant.

COMMUNITY SERVICE

Board Member, Oakland County Jaycees. September 1988-Present.

Member, Oakland County Big Brothers, September 1988-Present.

President, Kimberly Subdivision Neighborhood Watch, April 1989-April 1991.

1996 General Schedule
(Extract)

GRADE	STEP				
	1	**2**	**3**	**4**	**5**
GS-3	$ 15,820	$ 16,347	$ 16,874	$ 17,401	$ 17,928
-4	17,759	18,352	18,944	19,537	20,129
-5	19,869	20,531	21,194	21,856	22,518
-6	22,147	22,886	23,624	24,362	25,101
-7	24,610	25,431	26,251	27,072	27,892
-8	27,256	28,165	29,074	29,983	30,892
-9	30,106	31,110	32,114	33,118	34,121
-10	33,154	34,259	35,364	36,468	37,573
-11	36,426	37,640	38,854	40,068	41,282
-12	43,658	45,113	46,569	48,025	49,480

NOTES: (1) These figures include a "Rest of the U.S." locality payment of 4.1%. Annual rates for designated high-cost areas are slightly higher due to elevated locality payments ranging from a low of 4.38% to a high of 9.40% for specific areas. The high-cost areas include Atlanta, GA; Boston-Worcester-Lawrence, MA-NH-ME-CT; Chicago-Gary-Kenosha, IL-IN-WI; Cincinnati-Hamilton, OH-KY-IN; Cleveland-Akron, OH; Columbus, OH; Dallas-Fort Worth, TX; Dayton-Springfield, OH; Denver-Boulder-Greeley, CO; Detroit-Ann Arbor-Flint, MI; Houston-Galveston-Brazoria, TX; Huntsville, AL; Indianapolis, IN; Kansas City, MO-KS; Los Angeles-Riverside-Orange County, CA (including Santa Barbara County and all of Edwards Air Force Base); Miami-Fort Lauderdale, FL; New York-Northern New Jersey- Long Island, NY-NJ-CT-PA; Philadelphia-Wilmington-Atlantic City, PA-NJ-DE-MD; Port-land-Salem, OR-WA; Richmond-Petersburg, VA; Sacramento-Yolo, CA; St. Louis, MO-IL; San Diego, CA; San Francisco-Oakland-San Jose, CA; Seattle-Tacoma-Bremerton, WA; and Washington-Baltimore, DC-MD-VA-WV. (2) As of this writing, the 1997 General Schedule rates were not yet published.

Source: *Federal Employees News Digest*, on-line via *Infoseek*, October 5, 1996.

1997 Military Pay Schedule
(Extract)

GRADE	YEARS OF SERVICE				
	<u>≤2</u>	<u>2</u>	<u>3</u>	<u>4</u>	<u>6</u>
E-1	$10,811	$10,811	$10,811	$10,811	$10,811
E-2	12,121	12,121	12,121	12,121	12,121
E-3	12,596	13,284	13,813	14,360	14,360
E-4	13,363	14,116	14,947	16,099	16,736
E-5	14,332	15,599	16,355	17,068	18,191
O-1	20,711	21,553	26,050	26,050	26,050

NOTE: Additional allowances are paid for quarters and food when soldiers do not reside in government housing or dine in government facilities. Factors such as marital status and subsistence category affect the amount of the allowances, which can range from $5,460 per year for a single E-1 to $7,736 per year for a married 0-1.

Source: "The 1997 Army Times Pay Chart," *Army Times*, September 30, 1996.

1997 Executive and Administrative Schedule
(Extract)

SALARY RANGES

GRADE	MINIMUM	MID-POINT	MAXIMUM
EAS-17	$ 39,159	$ 45,425	$ 51,690
-18	40,879	47,419	53,960
-19	42,817	49,667	56,518
-20	45,140	52,363	59,585
-21	47,332	54,905	62,478
-22	49,902	57,887	65,871
-23	52,621	61,041	69,460

Appendix H

Sample Letters

1. REQUEST FOR AGENCY INFORMATION

JOHN J. DOE
12345 Main Street
Jackson, MS 12345
(123) 456-7890

September 30, 1996

Department of the Interior
Bureau of Indian Affairs
Division of Personnel Management
1951 Constitution Avenue, NW
Washington, DC 20240

Dear Sir or Madam:

I am interested in the opportunities available as a Criminal Investigator with the Bureau of Indian Affairs. Please forward information concerning specific qualifications, application procedures, a job description, and any other material that might be helpful in pursuit of this position, to the address indicated above.

Thank you for your assistance.

Sincerely,

John J. Doe

2. SUBMITTING AN APPLICATION

JOHN J. DOE
12345 Main Street
Jackson, MS 12345
(123) 456-7890

September 30, 1996

Department of the Interior
Bureau of Indian Affairs
Division of Personnel Management
1951 Constitution Avenue, NW
Washington, DC 20240

Dear Sir or Madam:

This letter forwards my application for the position of Criminal Investigator with the Bureau of Indian Affairs. The required application forms and a copy of my resume are enclosed.

I believe my qualifications are ideally suited to this position, and look forward to the opportunity for an interview. Thank you for considering my application.

Sincerely,

John J. Doe

Enclosures

3. SUBMITTING A RESUME

JOHN J. DOE
12345 Main Street
Jackson, MS 12345
(123) 456-7890

September 30, 1996

Brunswick Security
ATTN: Ms. Brenda Watkins
        Director of Human Resources
811 Billings Lane
Taylor, Michigan 48180

Dear Ms. Watkins:

This letter is submitted in response to your advertisement for the position of Security Team Leader at the Enrico Fermi Nuclear Power Plant. My resume is enclosed.

I believe my qualifications are ideally suited to this position, and look forward to the opportunity for an interview. Thank you for considering my application.

Sincerely,

John J. Doe

Enclosure

4. POST-INTERVIEW FOLLOW-UP

JOHN J. DOE
12345 Main Street
Jackson, MS 12345
(123) 456-7890

September 30, 1996

Brunswick Security
ATTN: Ms. Brenda Watkins
      Director of Human Resources
811 Billings Lane
Taylor, Michigan 48180

Dear Ms. Watkins:

Thank you for the opportunity to meet with you, Mr. Agajanian, and Mr. Wilhelm earlier today. The members of the interview panel, as well as the other employees I had the chance to speak with, made me feel welcome and comfortable throughout my visit. Your courtesy and consideration are greatly appreciated.

As I mentioned during our discussion, it is remarkable how closely Brunswick's job description for Security Team Leader so closely matches my four years of experience as a Security Squad Leader during military service. It was a job at which I excelled, as documented in the letters of reference which accompanied my original application. I am confident in my ability to consistently provide top-notch performance for you, too.

There is an air of collegiality, professionalism, and focus at Brunswick Security. It left me both impressed and enthused at the prospect of joining your team. I hope your impression of me was equally positive.

Thank you again for your courtesy. I look forward to hearing from you soon.

                           Sincerely,

                           John J. Doe

5. POST-REJECTION FOLLOW-UP

JOHN J. DOE
12345 Main Street
Jackson, MS 12345
(123) 456-7890

September 30, 1996

Brunswick Security
ATTN: Ms. Brenda Watkins
      Director of Human Resources
811 Billings Lane
Taylor, Michigan 48180

Dear Ms. Watkins:

Thank you for advising me of the status of my application for the position of Security Team Leader. While it was not the news I had hoped for, I remain enthusiastic at the possibility of eventually joining Brunswick Security in some future opening.

Although my qualifications did not meet your needs for this position, I know my skills would enable me to make significant contributions to Brunswick's operations. Please keep me in mind should a vacancy arise for which you might consider me better suited.

Thank you again for your courtesy.

Sincerely,

John J. Doe

Sample Completed SF-171

Application for Federal Employment—SF 171

Read the instructions before you complete this application. *Type or print clearly in dark ink.*

Form Approved
OMB No. 3206-00 2

GENERAL INFORMATION

1 What kind of job are you applying for? *Give title and announcement no. (if any)*

Administrative Officer
Announcement No. 123-456

2 Social Security Number
123-45-6789

3 Sex
[x] Male [ ] Female

4 Birth date *(Month, Day, Year)*
12-12-45

5 Birthplace *(City and State or Country)*
Simpson, Maine

6 Name *(Last, First, Middle)*
DOE, John Joseph

Mailing address *(include apartment number, if any)*
12345 Main Street

City: Jackson   State: MS   ZIP Code: 12345

7 Other names ever used *(e.g., maiden name, nickname, etc.)*
Not applicable

8 Home Phone
Area Code: 123   Number: 456-7890

9 Work Phone
Area Code: 123   Number: 789-0123   Extension:

10 Were you ever employed as a civilian by the Federal Government? If **"NO"**, go to Item 11. If **"YES"**, mark each type of job you held with an **"X"**. **No**

[ ] Temporary   [ ] Career-Conditional   [ ] Career   [ ] Excepted

What is your **highest** grade, classification series and job title?
Not applicable

Dates at **highest** grade: FROM N/A   TO N/A

FOR USE OF EXAMINING OFFICE ONLY

Date entered register | Form reviewed | Form approved:

Option	Grade	Earned Rating	Veteran Preference	Augmented Rating

[ ] No Preference Claimed
[ ] 5 Points (Tentative)
[ ] 10 Pts (30% Or More Comp. Dis.)
[ ] 10 Pts (Less Than 30% Comp. Dis.)
[ ] Other 10 Points

Initials and Date

[ ] Disallowed   [ ] Being Investigated

FOR USE OF APPOINTING OFFICE ONLY

Preference has been verified through proof that the separation was under honorable conditions, and other proof as required

[ ] 5-Point
[ ] 10-Point 30% or More Compensable Disability
[ ] 10-Point-Less Than 30% Compensable Disability
[ ] 10-Point Other

Signature and Title

Agency   Date

AVAILABILITY

11 When can you start work? *(Month and Year)*
12-93

12 What is the **lowest** pay you will accept? *(You will not be considered for jobs which pay less than you indicate.)*
Pay $ _____ per _____ OR Grade GS-9

13 In what geographic area(s) are you willing to work?
Worldwide

14 Are you willing to work:

	YES	NO
A. 40 hours per week *(full-time)*?	x	
B. 25-32 hours per week *(part-time)*?	x	
C. 17-24 hours per week *(part-time)*?	x	
D. 16 or fewer hours per week *(part-time)*?	x	
E. An intermittent job *(on-call/seasonal)*?	x	
F. Weekends, shifts, or rotating shifts?	x	

15 Are you willing to take a temporary job lasting:

	YES	NO
A. 5 to 12 months *(sometimes longer)*?	x	
B. 1 to 4 months?	x	
C. Less than 1 month?	x	

16 Are you willing to travel away from home for:

	YES	NO
A. 1 to 5 nights each month?	x	
B. 6 to 10 nights each month?	x	
C. 11 or more nights each month?	x	

MILITARY SERVICE AND VETERAN PREFERENCE

17 Have you served in the United States Military Service? *If your only active duty was training in the Reserves or National Guard, answer "NO". If "NO", go to item 22.*

YES	NO
x	

18 Did you or will you retire at or above the rank of major or lieutenant commander?

YES	NO
	x

THE FEDERAL GOVERNMENT IS AN EQUAL OPPORTUNITY EMPLOYER
PREVIOUS EDITION USABLE UNTIL 12-31-90

MILITARY SERVICE AND VETERAN PREFERENCE *(Cont.)*

19 Were you discharged from the military service under honorable conditions? *(If your discharge was changed to "honorable" or "general" by a Discharge Review Board, answer "YES". If you received a clemency discharge, answer "NO".)* If **"NO"**, provide below the date and type of discharge you received.

YES	NO
	x

Discharge Date *(Month, Day, Year)*	Type of Discharge
12-31-88	Honorable

20 List the dates *(Month, Day, Year)*, and branch for all **active duty** military service.

From	To	Branch of Service
08-10-67	08-09-71	U.S. Army

21 If all your active military duty was after October 14, 1976, list the full names and dates of all campaign badges or expeditionary medals you received or were entitled to receive.

Not applicable

22 Read the instructions that came with this form before completing this item. When you have determined your eligibility for veteran preference from the instructions, place an **"X"** in the box next to your veteran preference claim.

[ ] NO PREFERENCE
[x] 5-POINT PREFERENCE -- You must show proof when you are hired.

10-POINT PREFERENCE -- If you claim 10-point preference, place an **"X"** in the box below next to the basis for your claim. To receive 10-point preference you must also complete a Standard Form 15, Application for 10-Point Veteran Preference, which is available from any Federal Job Information Center. **ATTACH THE COMPLETED SF 15 AND REQUESTED PROOF TO THIS APPLICATION.**

[ ] Non-compensably disabled or Purple Heart recipient.
[ ] Compensably disabled, less than 30 percent.
[ ] Spouse, widow(er), or mother of a deceased or disabled veteran.
[ ] Compensably disabled, 30 percent or more.

NSN 7540-00-935-7150   171-110
Standard Form 171 (Rev 6-88)
U.S. Office of Personnel Management
FPM Chapter 295

Page 1

23 May we ask your present employer about your character, qualifications, and work record? A "NO" will not affect our review of your qualifications. If you answer "NO" and we need to contact your present employer before we can offer you a job, we will contact you first. . . . .

	YES	NO
		X

24 READ **WORK EXPERIENCE** IN THE INSTRUCTIONS BEFORE YOU BEGIN.

- Describe your current or most recent job in Block **A** and work backwards, describing each job you held **during the past 10 years.** If you were **unemployed** for longer than **3 months** within the past 10 years, list the dates and your address(es) in an experience block.

- You may sum up in one block work that you did **more than 10 years ago.** But if that work **is related** to the type of job you are applying for, describe each related job in a separate block.

- INCLUDE VOLUNTEER WORK *(non-paid work)*--**If the work** *(or a part of the work)* **is like the job you are applying for,** complete all parts of the experience block just as you would for a paying job. You may receive credit for work experience with religious, community, welfare, service, and other organizations.

- INCLUDE MILITARY SERVICE--You should complete all parts of the experience block just as you would for a non-military job. including all supervisory experience. Describe each major change of duties or responsibilities in a separate experience block.

- IF YOU NEED MORE SPACE TO DESCRIBE A JOB--Use sheets of paper the same size as this page (be sure to include all information we ask for in **A** and **B** below). On each sheet show your name, Social Security Number, and the announcement number or job title.

- IF YOU NEED MORE EXPERIENCE BLOCKS, use the SF 171-A or a sheet of paper.

- IF YOU NEED TO UPDATE (ADD MORE RECENT JOBS), use the SF 172 or a sheet of paper as described above.

A Name and address of employer's organization *(include ZIP Code, if known)*

Acme Manufacturing Company
9876 Oak Avenue
Jackson, MS 12345

Dates employed *(give month, day and year)*	Average number of hours per week	Number of employees you supervise
From: 07-19-87 To: **Present**	40	22

Salary or earnings		Your reason for wanting to leave
Starting $ 31,400 per year		Involuntary layoff
Ending $ 34,900 per year		(plant closing)

Your immediate supervisor			Exact title of your job	If Federal employment *(civilian or military)* list series, grade or rank, and, if promoted in this job, the date of your last promotion
Name	Area Code	Telephone No.		
J. Brownley	456	789-0123	Shift Supervisor	Not applicable

Description of work: Describe your specific duties, responsibilities and accomplishments in this job, **including** the job title(s) of any employees you supervise. *If you describe more than one* type of work *(for example, carpentry and painting, or personnel and budget), write the* approximate percentage of time you spent doing each.

Manage small sheet metal manufacturing process. Supervise a work force of 14 sheet metal workers, 4 technicians, 2 team leaders, and an administrative assistant. Responsible for planning, scheduling, coordinating, and resourcing production requirements to meet delivery due dates expected by customers. Prepare and submit production forecasts. Identify and resolve logistical obstacles to achievement of established deadlines. Maintain the serviceability of highly complex, state-of-the-art technical equipment and computer-integrated machinery. In coordination with the Personnel Officer, interview and evaluate candidates for employment.

For Agency Use (skill codes, etc.)

B Name and address of employer's organization *(include ZIP Code, if known)*

Reach-Out, Incorporated
23456 Elm Street
Jackson, MS 12345

Dates employed *(give month, day and year)*	Average number of hours per week	Number of employees you supervised
From: 09-11-87 To: **Present**	10	0

Salary or earnings		Your reason for leaving
Starting $ 0 per N/A		Not applicable
Ending $ 0 per N/A		

Your immediate supervisor			Exact title of your job	If Federal employment *(civilian or military)* list series, grade or rank, and, if promoted in this job, the date of your last promotion
Name	Area Code	Telephone No.		
Mr. K. Weir	123	369-2468	Volunteer Counselor	Not applicable

Description of work: Describe your specific duties, responsibilities and accomplishments in this job, **including** the job title(s) of any employees you supervised. *If you describe more than one* type of work *(for example, carpentry and painting, or personnel and budget), write the* approximate percentage of time you spent doing each.

Serve as a volunteer Crisis Intervention Counselor to assist troubled youth in coping with home and family crises. Meet with youths referred by law enforcement, church, or other social agencies, or who seek counseling on their own volition. Mediate disputes with family members, schoolmates, co-workers or friends. Assist youths in understanding difficult life events, such as parental divorce, deaths in the family, or other emotionally difficult experiences. Coordinate the intervention of various social assistance groups, as appropriate.

For Agency Use (skill codes, etc.)

Page 2   IF YOU NEED MORE EXPERIENCE BLOCKS, USE SF 171-A *(SEE BACK OF INSTRUCTION PAGE).*

Standard Form 171-A— *Continuation Sheet for SF 171 (Back)*

● Attach all SF 171-A's to your application at the top of page 3.

1. Name *(Last, First, Middle Initial)* DOE, John J.	2. Social Security Number 123-45-6789
3. Job Title or Announcement Number You Are Applying For Administrative Officer, Announcement No. 123-456	4. Date Completed 05-31-93

ADDITIONAL WORK EXPERIENCE BLOCKS

C

Name and address of employer's organization *(include ZIP Code, if known)* AWR Associates P.O. Box 8885 Lawrence, KS 66046	Dates employed *(give month, day and year)* From: 11-26-75 To: 07-18-87 Salary or earnings Starting $ 26,925 per year Ending $ 34,695 per year	Average number of hours per week 40	Number of employees you supervised 28
		Your reason for leaving Company lost contract renewal bid.	

Your immediate supervisor			If Federal employment *(civilian or military)* list series, grade or rank, and, if promoted in this job, the date of your last promotion
Name M.S. Peyton	Area Code Telephone No. 913 841-0000	Exact title of your job Project Manager	Not applicable

Description of work: Describe your specific duties, responsibilities and accomplishments in this job, **including** the job title(s) of any employees you supervised. *If you describe more than one type of work (for example, carpentry and painting, or personnel and budget), write the approximate percentage of time you spent doing each.*

Supervised 28 administrative and training specialists providing educational services support to a population of more than 100,000 soldiers and civilians at Fort Bragg, North Carolina. Initiated program start-up activities under a newly awarded U.S. Government contract, including hiring and training the work force, and coordinating the acquisition of facilities and equipment to support program requirements and performance objectives. As Contractor Representative, resolved all matters relating to contract compliance and performance assessment, and negotiated contract modifications.

Performed all aspects of Human Resource operations, including recruitment, interviewing, testing, background verification, hiring/firing, policy development, training, employee relations, performance evaluation and counseling, benefits and compensation, payroll, safety, implementation and administration of Affirmative Action and Equal Employment Opportunity programs, and compliance with applicable state and federal employment requirements.

Managed seven test sites administering more than 500,000 standardized and specialized tests each year, including the General Educational Development series, the Armed Services Vocational Aptitude Battery, the College Level Examination Program tests, the Scholastic Aptitude Test, the Graduate Record Examination, the General Management Aptitude Test, the Career Assessment Inventory, varied specialized tests, and course examinations for supported satellite campuses of major educational institutions serving the Fort Bragg community. Responsible for security of classified testing materials and sites, and the integrity of testing operations.

Managed five technical libraries providing reference material support in print, audio, video, and computer data formats. Responsible for maintaining the currency and accuracy of 200,000 + reference sources at each library site.

Managed one language training and testing facility providing linguistic support in more than 90 languages and dialects. Trained soldiers to high levels of ability in reading, comprehending, and speaking specified languages. Administered more than 250,000 qualification and competency tests annually, in both written and oral formats.

Managed space utilization, facilities maintenance, and physical plant operations for one main office facility, seven testing centers, five library sites, and one language training/testing complex.

Responsible for the serviceability, maintenance, accountability and utilization of facilities and equipment valued in excess of $2.5 million.

Managed a $600,000 annual budget.

For Agency Use (skill codes, etc.)

●U.S. Government Printing Office: 1990-262-081/90304

Standard Form 171-A (BACK) (Rev 6-88)
U.S. Office of Personnel Management
FPM Chapter 295

Standard Form 171-A— *Continuation Sheet for SF 171*

Form Approved
OMB No 3206-0012

• Attach all SF 171-A's to your application at the top of page 3.

1. Name *(Last, First, Middle Initial)*	2. Social Security Number
DOE, John J.	369-46-4776

3. Job Title or Announcement Number You Are Applying For	4. Date Completed
Administrative Officer, Announcement No. 123-456	05-31-93

ADDITIONAL WORK EXPERIENCE BLOCKS

D

Name and address of employer's organization *(include ZIP Code, if known)*	Dates employed *(give month, day and year)*	Average number of hours per week	Number of employees you supervised
Unemployed	From: 05-28-75 To: 11-25-75	60	0

Salary or earnings	Your reason for leaving
Starting $ per	
Ending $ per	

Your immediate supervisor	Exact title of your job	If Federal employment *(civilian or military)* list series, grade or rank, and, if promoted in this job, the date of your last promotion
Name Area Code Telephone No.		
Not applicable		

Description of work: Describe your specific duties, responsibilities and accomplishments in this job, including the job title(s) of any employees you supervised. *If you describe more than one type of work (for example, carpentry and painting, or personnel and budget), write the approximate percentage of time you spent doing each.*

Conducted job search activities to identify and obtain employment.

For Agency Use (skill codes, etc.)

E

Name and address of employer's organization *(include ZIP Code, if known)*	Dates employed *(give month, day and year)*	Average number of hours per week	Number of employees you supervised
Columbia College Columbia, MO 66036	From: 09-04-71 To: 05-27-75	60	0

Salary or earnings	Your reason for leaving
Starting $ 0 per year	Graduated.
Ending $ 0 per year	

Your immediate supervisor	Exact title of your job	If Federal employment *(civilian or military)* list series, grade or rank, and, if promoted in this job, the date of your last promotion
Name Area Code Telephone No.		
C. Able, Ph.D Unknown Student		Not applicable

Description of work: Describe your specific duties, responsibilities and accomplishments in this job, including the job title(s) of any employees you supervised. *If you describe more than one type of work (for example, carpentry and painting, or personnel and budget), write the approximate percentage of time you spent doing each.*

As a Business Administration major, studied entry-level business management systems and processes employed in the accomplishment of normal business operations. Took a minor in Education.

For Agency Use (skill codes, etc.)

Standard Form 171-A (Rev. 6-88)
U.S. Office of Personnel Management
FPM Chapter 295

Standard Form 171-A— *Continuation Sheet for SF 171 (Back)*

• Attach all SF 171-A's to your application at the top of page 3.

1. Name *(Last, First, Middle Initial)*	2. Social Security Number
DOE, JOHN J.	123-45-6789

3. Job Title or Announcement Number You Are Applying For	4. Date Completed
Administrative Officer, Announcement No. 123-456	05-31-93

ADDITIONAL WORK EXPERIENCE BLOCKS

F	Name and address of employer's organization *(include ZIP Code, if known)*	Dates employed *(give month, day and year)*	Average number of hours per week	Number of employees you supervised
	U.S. Army Headquarters, Combined Field Army (Republic of Korea/United States) APO San Francisco 96358	From: 08-10-67 To: 08-09-71	60	440

Salary or earnings		Your reason for leaving
Starting $ 7,915 per year		Discharged from
Ending $ 19,328 per year		active duty.

Your immediate supervisor		Exact title of your job	If Federal employment *(civilian or military)* list series, grade or rank, and, if promoted in this job, the date of your last promotion
Name Colonel W. Johnson	Area Code Telephone No. Unknown	Company Commander	Captain, O-3

Description of work: Describe your specific duties, responsibilities and accomplishments in this job, **including** the job title(s) of any employees you supervised. *If you describe more than one type of work (for example, carpentry and painting, or personnel and budget), write the approximate percentage of time you spent doing each.*

CIVILIAN TITLE: General Manager.

Completed entry-level training from 08-10-67 through 09-14-68, followed by assignment to the Republic of Korea. Performed a variety of developmental junior officer duty assignments, culminating with appointment to command the company.

Assisted by 5 junior officers, commanded a 19-member support staff and 420 U.S. and Korean National employees executing all human resource, administrative, intelligence analysis, tactical planning and operations, logistical, maintenance, and civil/military affairs missions in the Republic of Korea-based headquarters of the largest field army in the free world.

Managed all human resource programs, including compliance with federal Equal Employment Opportunity and Affirmative Action Plan guidelines; personnel policy formulation; staffing analysis; preparation of position descriptions and justifications for modifications of manning authorization levels; labor relations; grievance resolution; U.S. Congressional inquiry response; awards, incentives, and morale; discipline; alcohol/drug abuse prevention and control; employee retention; employee orientation; safety; finance and payroll services; employee counseling; job performance evaluation; job skill testing, training, and development; physical training; recreational services; quality of life; medical services; vacation program management; and survivor assistance.

Managed all administrative service programs, including files and records management; postal operations; internal and external distribution services; publications library services; word processing center operations; and preparation of all executive correspondence.

Managed the dispatch, use, and maintenance of a 220-vehicle transportation fleet consisting of sedans, light- and heavy-duty trucks, vans, buses, trailers, combat vehicles, maintenance wreckers, and power generation equipment.

Managed space utilization, facilities maintenance, and physical plant operations for one headquarters office complex, four equipment warehouses, one food preparation/storage kitchen with an attached 300-seat dining facility, one high-security arms storage facility, one high-security mail room, one motor vehicle maintenance garage and motor park, and fourteen single- and multi-floor dormitories.

Responsible for the serviceability, maintenance, accountability and utilization of facilities and equipment valued in excess of $23 million.

Managed an $840,000 annual budget. Prepared budget projections for all company activities. Submitted and defended annual budget input.

For Agency Use (skill codes, etc.)

* U.S. Government Printing Office: 1990-262-081/90304

Standard Form 171-A (BACK) (Rev 6-88)
U.S. Office of Personnel Management
FPM Chapter 295

EDUCATION

25 Did you graduate from high school? *If you have a GED high school equivalency or will graduate within the next nine months, answer "YES".*

26 Write the name and location *(city and state)* of the last high school you attended or where you obtained your GED high school equivalency.

North Farmington HS, Farmington Hills, MI

YES **x** — If "YES", give month and year graduated or received GED equivalency: 06-71

NO — If "NO", give the highest grade you completed: .

27 Have you ever attended college or graduate school? YES **x** If "YES", continue with 28. NO If NO", go to 31.

28 NAME AND LOCATION *(city, state and ZIP Code)* OF COLLEGE OR UNIVERSITY. *If you expect to graduate within nine months, give the month and year you expect to receive your degree:*

	Name	City	State	ZIP Code	MONTH AND YEAR ATTENDED From	To	NUMBER OF CREDIT HOURS COMPLETED Semester	Quarter	TYPE OF DEGREE *(e.g. B.A. M.A.)*	MONTH AND YEAR OF DEGREE
1)	Columbia College	Columbia	M O	6 6 0 3 6	09-71	05-75	121		B.A.	10-75
2)										
3)										

29 CHIEF UNDERGRADUATE SUBJECTS — *Show major on the first line*

		NUMBER OF CREDIT HOURS COMPLETED Semester	Quarter
1)	Business Administration	45	
2)	Education	24	
3)			

30 CHIEF GRADUATE SUBJECTS — *Show major on the first line*

		NUMBER OF CREDIT HOURS COMPLETED Semester	Quarter
1)	Not applicable		
2)			
3)			

31 If you have completed any **other courses or training** related to the kind of jobs you are applying for *(trade, vocational, Armed Forces, business)* give information below.

NAME AND LOCATION *(city, state and ZIP Code)* OF SCHOOL	MONTH AND YEAR ATTENDED From	To	CLASS-ROOM HOURS	SUBJECT(S)	TRAINING COMPLETED YES NO
School Name 1) Not applicable. City State ZIP Code					
School Name 2) City State ZIP Code					

SPECIAL SKILLS, ACCOMPLISHMENTS AND AWARDS

32 Give the title and year of any honors, awards or fellowships you have received. List your special qualifications, skills or accomplishments that may help you get a job. *Some examples are: skills with computers or other machines; most important publications (do not submit copies); public speaking and writing experience; membership in professional or scientific societies; patents or inventions; etc.*

a. As a member of Toastmasters, International, I give monthly speeches on a variety of subjects to the assembled membership of approximately 100 businessmen. b. Through the use of my home personal computer, I have developed strong computer skills and have become highly skilled in a wide variety of softwares, including Windows, Word for Windows, and LOTUS 1-2-3.

33 How many words per minute can you:

TYPE?	TAKE DICTATION?
45	0

Agencies may test your skills before hiring you.

34 List **job-related** licenses or certificates that you have, such as: *registered nurse; lawyer; radio operator; driver's; pilot's; etc.*

	LICENSE OR CERTIFICATE	DATE OF LATEST LICENSE OR CERTIFICATE	STATE OR OTHER LICENSING AGENCY
1)	Not applicable		
2)			

35 Do you speak or read a language other than English *(include sign language)?* *Applicants for jobs that require a language other than English may be given an interview conducted solely in that language.* YES / NO **x** — If "YES", list each language and place an "X" in each column that applies to you. If "NO", go to 36.

LANGUAGE(S)	CAN PREPARE AND GIVE LECTURES Fluently	With Difficulty	CAN SPEAK AND UNDERSTAND Fluently	Passably	CAN TRANSLATE ARTICLES Into English	From English	CAN READ ARTICLES FOR OWN USE Easily	With Difficulty
1) Not applicable								
2)								

REFERENCES

36 List three people who are not related to you and are not supervisors you listed under 24 who know your qualifications and fitness for the kind of job for which you are applying. At least **one** should know you well on a personal basis.

	FULL NAME OF REFERENCE	TELEPHONE NUMBER(S) *(Include Area Code)*	PRESENT BUSINESS OR HOME ADDRESS *(Number, street and city)*	STATE	ZIP CODE
1)	Frank Johnson	(919) 738-2584	629 Mangrove Rd. Lumberton	N C	2 8 3 5 8
2)	Robert Kelly	(123) 436-0014	516 Thorn St. Fayetteville	M S	2 4 6 8 0
3)	F.J. Swanson	(123) 484-4433	3139 Hill Ave. Fayetteville	M S	2 4 6 8 0

Page 3

37 Are you a citizen of the United States? *(In most cases you must be a U.S. citizen to be hired. You will be required to submit proof of identity and citizenship at the time you are hired.)* If **"NO"**, give the country or countries you are a citizen of: _____

YES   NO
    X

> **NOTE:** It is important that you give complete and truthful answers to questions 38 through 44. If you answer **"YES"** to any of them, provide your explanation(s) in **Item 45. Include** convictions resulting from a plea of nolo contendere *(no contest).* Omit: 1) traffic fines of $100.00 or less: 2) any violation of law committed before your 16th birthday; 3) any violation of law committed before your 18th birthday, if finally decided in juvenile court or under a Youth Offender law; 4) any conviction set aside under the Federal Youth Corrections Act or similar State law; 5) any conviction whose record was expunged under Federal or State law. We will consider the date, facts, and circumstances of each event you list. In most cases you can still be considered for Federal jobs. However, **if you fail to tell the truth or fail to list all relevant** events or circumstances, this may be grounds for not hiring you, for firing you after you begin work, or for criminal prosecution (18 USC 1001).

		YES	NO
38	During the last **10 years**, were you **fired from any job** for any reason, did you **quit after being told that you would be fired**, or did you leave by mutual agreement because of specific problems?.		X
39	Have you **ever** been convicted of, or forfeited collateral for **any felony violation?** *(Generally, a felony is defined as any violation of law punishable by imprisonment of longer than one year, except for violations called misdemeanors under State law which are punishable by imprisonment of two years or less.)*		X
40	Have you **ever** been convicted of, or forfeited collateral for **any firearms or explosives violation?**		X
41	Are you **now** under charges for **any** violation of law?		X
42	During the **last 10 years** have you forfeited collateral, been convicted, been imprisoned, been on probation, or been on parole? Do **not** include violations reported in 39, 40, or 41, above.		X
43	Have you **ever** been convicted by a military **court-martial?** If no military service, answer, **"NO".**		X
44	Are you **delinquent** on any Federal debt? *(Include delinquencies arising from Federal taxes, loans, overpayment of benefits, and other debts to the U.S. Government **plus** defaults on Federally guaranteed or insured loans such as student and home mortgage loans.)*		X

45 If **"YES"** in: **38** - Explain for each job the problem(s) and your reason(s) for leaving. Give the employer's name and address.
        39 through 43 - Explain each violation. Give place of occurrence and name/address of police or court involved.
        44 - Explain the type, length and amount of the delinquency or default, and steps you are taking to correct errors or repay the debt. Give any identification number associated with the debt and the address of the Federal agency involved.
    NOTE: If you need more space, use a sheet of paper, and include the item number.

Item No.	Date (Mo./Yr.)	Explanation	Mailing Address
		Not applicable	Name of Employer, Police, Court, or Federal Agency City State ZIP Code
			Name of Employer, Police, Court, or Federal Agency City State ZIP Code

46 Do you receive, or have you ever applied for retirement pay, pension, or other pay based on military, Federal civilian, or District of Columbia Government service? . . . .

YES   NO
    X

47 Do any of your relatives work for the United States Government or the United States Armed Forces? Include: *father; mother; husband; wife; son; daughter; brother; sister; uncle; aunt; first cousin; nephew; niece; father-in-law; mother-in-law; son-in-law; daughter-in-law; brother-in-law; sister-in-law; stepfather; stepmother; stepson; stepdaughter; stepbrother; stepsister; half brother; and half sister.* . . . .
If **"YES"**, provide details below. If you need more space, use a sheet of paper.

YES
    X

Name	Relationship	Department, Agency or Branch of Armed Forces
SMITH, Wanda L.	Niece	U.S. Marine Corps

SIGNATURE, CERTIFICATION, AND RELEASE OF INFORMATION

YOU MUST SIGN THIS APPLICATION. Read the following carefully before you sign.

- A false statement on any part of your application may be grounds for not hiring you, or for firing you after you begin work. Also, you may be punished by fine or imprisonment (U.S. Code, title 18, section 1001).
- If you are a male born after December 31, 1959 you must be registered with the Selective Service System or have a valid exemption in order to be eligible for Federal employment. You will be required to certify as to your status at the time of appointment.
- **I understand** that any information I give may be investigated as allowed by law or Presidential order.
- **I consent** to the release of information about my ability and fitness for Federal employment by *employers, schools, law enforcement agencies and other individuals and organizations,* to *investigators, personnel staffing specialists, and other authorized employees of the Federal Government.*
- **I certify** that, to the best of my knowledge and belief, **all** of my statements are true, correct, complete, and made in good faith.

48 SIGNATURE *(Sign each application in dark ink)*	**49** DATE SIGNED *(Month, day, year)*

* U.S. Government Printing Office: 1989-262-28/

Application for Federal Employment—SF 171

Read the instructions before you complete this application. *Type or print clearly in dark ink.*

Form Approved
OMB No. 3206-0012

GENERAL INFORMATION

1 What kind of job are you applying for? *Give title and announcement no. (if any)*

2 Social Security Number

3 Sex
☐ Male ☐ Female

4 Birth date *(Month, Day, Year)*

5 Birthplace *(City and State or Country)*

6 Name *(Last, First, Middle)*

Mailing address *(include apartment number, if any)*

City   State   ZIP Code

7 Other names ever used *(e.g., maiden name, nickname, etc.)*

8 Home Phone
Area Code | Number

9 Work Phone
Area Code | Number | Extension

10 Were you ever employed as a civilian by the Federal Government? If **"NO"**, go to Item 11. If **"YES"**, mark each type of job you held with an **"X"**.

☐ Temporary ☐ Career-Conditional ☐ Career ☐ Excepted

What is your **highest** grade, classification series and job title?

Dates at **highest** grade: FROM   TO

FOR USE OF EXAMINING OFFICE ONLY

Date entered register

Form reviewed:
Form approved:

Option	Grade	Earned Rating	Veteran Preference	Augmented Rating
			☐ No Preference Claimed	
			☐ 5 Points *(Tentative)*	
			☐ 10 Pts. *(30% Or More Comp. Dis.)*	
			☐ 10 Pts. *(Less Than 30% Comp. Dis.)*	
			☐ Other 10 Points	

Initials and Date

☐ Disallowed | ☐ Being Investigated

FOR USE OF APPOINTING OFFICE ONLY

Preference has been verified through proof that the separation was under honorable conditions, and other proof as required.

☐ 5-Point ☐ 10-Point--30% or More Compensable Disability ☐ 10-Point--Less Than 30% Compensable Disability ☐ 10-Point--Other

Signature and Title

Agency | Date

AVAILABILITY

11 When can you start work? *(Month and Year)*

12 What is the **lowest** pay you will accept? *(You will not be considered for jobs which pay less than you indicate.)*

Pay $ _____ per _____ OR Grade _____

13 In what geographic area(s) are you willing to work?

14 Are you willing to work:

	YES	NO
A. 40 hours per week *(full-time)*?		
B. 25-32 hours per week *(part-time)*?		
C. 17-24 hours per week *(part-time)*?		
D. 16 or fewer hours per week *(part-time)*?		
E. An intermittent job *(on-call/seasonal)*?		
F. Weekends, shifts, or rotating shifts?		

15 Are you willing to take a temporary job lasting:

A. 5 to 12 months *(sometimes longer)*?
B. 1 to 4 months?
C. Less than 1 month?

16 Are you willing to travel away from home for:

A. 1 to 5 nights each month?
B. 6 to 10 nights each month?
C. 11 or more nights each month?

MILITARY SERVICE AND VETERAN PREFERENCE

17 Have you served in the United States Military Service? *If your only active duty was training in the Reserves or National Guard, answer "NO". If "NO", go to item 22.*

YES	NO

18 Did you or will you retire at or above the rank of major or lieutenant commander?

MILITARY SERVICE AND VETERAN PREFERENCE *(Cont.)*

19 Were you discharged from the military service under honorable conditions? *(If your discharge was changed to "honorable" or "general" by a Discharge Review Board, answer "YES". If you received a clemency discharge, answer "NO".)*
If **"NO"**, provide below the date and type of discharge you received.

YES	NO

Discharge Date *(Month, Day, Year)*	Type of Discharge

20 List the dates *(Month, Day, Year)*, and branch for all **active duty** military service.

From	To	Branch of Service

21 If all your active military duty was after October 14, 1976, list the full names and dates of all campaign badges or expeditionary medals you received or were entitled to receive.

22 Read the instructions that came with this form before completing this item. When you have determined your eligibility for veteran preference from the instructions, place an **"X"** in the box next to your veteran preference claim.

☐ NO PREFERENCE
☐ 5-POINT PREFERENCE -- You must show proof when you are hired.

10-POINT PREFERENCE -- If you claim 10-point preference, place an **"X"** in the box below next to the basis for your claim. **To receive 10-point preference you must also complete a Standard Form 15, Application for 10-Point Veteran Preference, which is available from any Federal Job Information Center. ATTACH THE COMPLETED SF 15 AND REQUESTED PROOF TO THIS APPLICATION.**

☐ Non-compensably disabled or Purple Heart recipient.
☐ Compensably disabled, less than 30 percent.
☐ Spouse, widow(er), or mother of a deceased or disabled veteran.
☐ Compensably disabled, 30 percent or more.

THE FEDERAL GOVERNMENT IS AN EQUAL OPPORTUNITY EMPLOYER
PREVIOUS EDITION USABLE UNTIL 12-31-90

NSN 7540-00-935-7150   171-110

Standard Form 171 (Rev. 6-88)
U.S. Office of Personnel Management
FPM Chapter 295

WORK EXPERIENCE *If you have no work experience, write "NONE" in A below and go to 25 on page 3.*

23 May we ask your present employer about your character, qualifications, and work record? A "NO" will not affect our review of your qualifications. If you answer "NO" and we need to contact your present employer before we can offer you a job, we will contact you first. . . . .

	YES	NO

24 READ **WORK EXPERIENCE** IN THE INSTRUCTIONS BEFORE YOU BEGIN.

- Describe your current or most recent job in Block **A** and work backwards, describing each job you held **during the past 10 years.** If you were **unemployed** for longer than **3 months** within the past 10 years, list the dates and your address(es) in an experience block.

- You may sum up in one block work that you did **more than 10 years ago.** But if that work **is related** to the type of job you are applying for, describe each related job in a separate block.

- INCLUDE VOLUNTEER WORK *(non-paid work)*--**If the work** *(or a part of the work)* **is like the job you are applying for,** complete **all** parts of the experience block just as you would for a paying job. You may receive credit for work experience with religious, community, welfare, service, and other organizations.

- INCLUDE MILITARY SERVICE--You should complete **all** parts of the experience block just as you would for a non-military job, including all supervisory experience. Describe each major change of duties or responsibilities in a separate experience block.

- IF YOU NEED MORE SPACE TO DESCRIBE A JOB--Use sheets of paper the same size as this page (be sure to include **all** information we ask for in **A** and **B** below). On **each** sheet show your name, Social Security Number, and the announcement number or job title.

- IF YOU NEED MORE EXPERIENCE BLOCKS, use the SF 171-A or a sheet of paper.

- IF YOU NEED TO UPDATE (ADD MORE RECENT JOBS), use the SF 172 or a sheet of paper as described above.

A Name and address of employer's organization *(include ZIP Code, if known)*

Dates employed *(give month, day and year)* From: To:
Salary or earnings Starting $ per Ending $ per
Average number of hours per week
Number of employees you supervise
Your reason for wanting to leave

Your immediate supervisor Name | Area Code | Telephone No. | Exact title of your job | If Federal employment *(civilian or military)* list series, grade or rank, and, if promoted in this job, the date of your last promotion

Description of work: Describe your specific duties, responsibilities and accomplishments in this job, **including** the job title(s) of any employees you supervise. If you describe more than one type of work (for example, carpentry and painting, or personnel and budget), write the approximate percentage of time you spent doing each.

For Agency Use (skill codes, etc.)

B Name and address of employer's organization *(include ZIP Code, if known)*

Dates employed *(give month, day and year)* From: To:
Salary or earnings Starting $ per Ending $ per
Average number of hours per week
Number of employees you supervised
Your reason for leaving

Your immediate supervisor Name | Area Code | Telephone No. | Exact title of your job | If Federal employment *(civilian or military)* list series, grade or rank, and, if promoted in this job, the date of your last promotion

Description of work: Describe your specific duties, responsibilities and accomplishments in this job, **including** the job title(s) of any employees you supervised. If you describe more than one type of work (for example, carpentry and painting, or personnel and budget), write the approximate percentage of time you spent doing each.

For Agency Use (skill codes, etc.)

EDUCATION

25 Did you graduate from high school? *If you have a GED high school equivalency or will graduate within the next nine months, answer "YES".*

26 Write the name and location *(city and state)* of the last high school you attended or where you obtained your GED high school equivalency.

YES — If "YES", give month and year graduated or received GED equivalency: ....
NO — If "NO", give the highest grade you completed: .

27 Have you ever attended college or graduate school?
YES — If "YES", continue with **28**.
NO — If "NO", go to **31**.

28 NAME AND LOCATION *(city, state and ZIP Code)* OF COLLEGE OR UNIVERSITY.. *If you expect to graduate within nine months, give the* **month** *and* **year** *you expect to receive your degree:*

Name	City	State	ZIP Code	MONTH AND YEAR ATTENDED From	To	NUMBER OF CREDIT HOURS COMPLETED Semester	Quarter	TYPE OF DEGREE *(e.g. B.A., M.A.)*	MONTH AND YEAR OF DEGREE
1)									
2)									
3)									

29 CHIEF UNDERGRADUATE SUBJECTS *Show major on the first line*

	NUMBER OF CREDIT HOURS COMPLETED Semester	Quarter
1)		
2)		
3)		

30 CHIEF GRADUATE SUBJECTS *Show major on the first line*

	NUMBER OF CREDIT HOURS COMPLETED Semester	Quarter
1)		
2)		
3)		

31 If you have completed any **other courses or training related to the kind of jobs you are applying for** *(trade, vocational, Armed Forces, business)* give information below.

NAME AND LOCATION *(city, state and ZIP Code)* OF SCHOOL	MONTH AND YEAR ATTENDED From	To	CLASS-ROOM HOURS	SUBJECT(S)	TRAINING COMPLETED YES	NO
School Name 1) City State ZIP Code						
School Name 2) City State ZIP Code						

SPECIAL SKILLS, ACCOMPLISHMENTS AND AWARDS

32 Give the title and year of any honors, awards or fellowships you have received. List your special qualifications, skills or accomplishments that may help you get a job. *Some examples are: skills with computers or other machines; most important publications (do not submit copies); public speaking and writing experience; membership in professional or scientific societies; patents or inventions; etc.*

33 How many words per minute can you: TYPE? TAKE DICTATION?
Agencies may test your skills before hiring you.

34 List **job-related** licenses or certificates that you have, such as: *registered nurse; lawyer; radio operator; driver's; pilot's; etc.*

LICENSE OR CERTIFICATE	DATE OF LATEST LICENSE OR CERTIFICATE	STATE OR OTHER LICENSING AGENCY
1)		
2)		

35 Do you speak or read a language other than English *(include sign language)?* **Applicants for jobs that require a language other than English may be given an interview conducted solely in that language.**
YES — If "YES", list each language and place an "X" in each column that applies to you.
NO — If "NO", go to **36**.

LANGUAGE(S)	CAN PREPARE AND GIVE LECTURES Fluently	With Difficulty	CAN SPEAK AND UNDERSTAND Fluently	Passably	CAN TRANSLATE ARTICLES Into English	From English	CAN READ ARTICLES FOR OWN USE Easily	With Difficulty
1)								
2)								

REFERENCES

36 List three people who are not related to you and are not supervisors you listed under **24** who know your qualifications and fitness for the kind of job for which you are applying. At least **one** should know you well on a personal basis.

FULL NAME OF REFERENCE	TELEPHONE NUMBER(S) *(Include Area Code)*	PRESENT BUSINESS OR HOME ADDRESS *(Number, street and city)*	STATE	ZIP CODE
1)				
2)				
3)				

Page 3

37 Are you a citizen of the United States? *(In most cases you must be a U.S. citizen to be hired. You will be required to submit proof of identity and citizenship at the time you are hired.)* If **"NO"**, give the country or countries you are a citizen of: _____ | YES | NO |

> **NOTE: It is important that you give complete and truthful answers to questions 38 through 44.** If you answer **"YES"** to any of them, provide your explanation(s) in **Item 45. Include** convictions resulting from a plea of nolo contendere *(no contest)*. **Omit:** 1) traffic fines of $100.00 or less; 2) any violation of law committed before your 16th birthday; 3) any violation of law committed before your 18th birthday, if finally decided in juvenile court or under a Youth Offender law; 4) any conviction set aside under the Federal Youth Corrections Act or similar State law; 5) any conviction whose record was expunged under Federal or State law. We will consider the date, facts, and circumstances of each event you list. In most cases you can still be considered for Federal jobs. However, **if you fail to tell the truth or fail to list all relevant** events or circumstances, this may be grounds for not hiring you, for firing you after you begin work, or for criminal prosecution (18 USC 1001).

38 During the last **10 years**, were you **fired from any job** for any reason, did you **quit after being told that you would be fired**, or did you leave by mutual agreement because of specific problems?.................................... | YES | NO |

39 Have you **ever** been convicted of, or forfeited collateral for **any felony violation?** *(Generally, a felony is defined as any violation of law punishable by imprisonment of longer than one year, except for violations called misdemeanors under State law which are punishable by imprisonment of two years or less.)* ....

40 Have you **ever** been convicted of, or forfeited collateral for **any firearms or explosives violation?** ....

41 Are you **now** under charges for **any** violation of law? ....

42 During the **last 10 years** have you forfeited collateral, been convicted, been imprisoned, been on probation, or been on parole? Do **not** include violations reported in 39, 40, or 41, above. ....

43 Have you **ever** been convicted by a military **court-martial?** If no military service, answer **"NO"**....................................

44 Are you **delinquent** on any Federal debt? *(Include delinquencies arising from Federal taxes, loans, overpayment of benefits, and other debts to the U.S. Government plus defaults on Federally guaranteed or insured loans such as student and home mortgage loans.)* ....

45 If **"YES"** in: 38 - Explain for each job the problem(s) and your reason(s) for leaving. Give the employer's name and address.
 39 through 43 - Explain each violation. Give place of occurrence and name/address of police or court involved.
 44 - Explain the type, length and amount of the delinquency or default, and steps you are taking to correct errors or repay the debt. Give any identification number associated with the debt and the address of the Federal agency involved.
 NOTE: If you need more space, use a sheet of paper, and include the item number.

Item No.	Date (Mo./Yr.)	Explanation	Mailing Address
			Name of Employer, Police, Court, or Federal Agency
			City State ZIP Code
			Name of Employer, Police, Court, or Federal Agency
			City State ZIP Code

46 Do you receive, or have you ever applied for retirement pay, pension, or other pay based on military, Federal civilian, or District of Columbia Government service? .... | YES | NO |

47 Do any of your relatives work for the United States Government or the United States Armed Forces? Include: *father; mother; husband; wife; son; daughter; brother; sister; uncle; aunt; first cousin; nephew; niece; father-in-law; mother-in-law; son-in-law; daughter-in-law; brother-in-law; sister-in-law; stepfather; stepmother; stepson; stepdaughter; stepbrother; stepsister; half brother; and half sister.* ....
If **"YES"**, provide details below. If you need more space, use a sheet of paper.

Name	Relationship	Department, Agency or Branch of Armed Forces

SIGNATURE, CERTIFICATION, AND RELEASE OF INFORMATION

YOU MUST SIGN THIS APPLICATION. Read the following carefully before you sign.

- A false statement on any part of your application may be grounds for not hiring you, or for firing you after you begin work. Also, you may be punished by fine or imprisonment (U.S. Code, title 18, section 1001).
- If you are a male born after December 31, 1959 you must be registered with the Selective Service System or have a valid exemption in order to be eligible for Federal employment. You will be required to certify as to your status at the time of appointment.
- **I understand** that any information I give may be investigated as allowed by law or Presidential order.
- **I consent** to the release of information about my ability and fitness for Federal employment by *employers, schools, law enforcement agencies and other individuals and organizations,* to *investigators, personnel staffing specialists, and other authorized employees of the Federal Government.*
- **I certify** that, to the best of my knowledge and belief, all of my statements are true, correct, complete, and made in good faith.

48 SIGNATURE *(Sign each application in dark ink)* | **49** DATE SIGNED *(Month, day, year)*

*U.S. Government Printing Office: 1992 — 342-199/50136

Standard Form 171-A— *Continuation Sheet for SF 171*

Form Approved.
OMB No. 3206-0012

• Attach all SF 171-A's to your application at the top of page 3.

1. Name *(Last, First, Middle Initial)*	2. Social Security Number

3. Job Title or Announcement Number You Are Applying For	4. Date Completed

ADDITIONAL WORK EXPERIENCE BLOCKS

☐ Name and address of employer's organization *(include ZIP Code, if known)*	Dates employed *(give month, day and year)*	Average number of hours per week	Number of employees you supervised
	From: To:		
	Salary or earnings	Your reason for leaving	
	Starting $ per		
	Ending $ per		

Your immediate supervisor			Exact title of your job	If Federal employment *(civilian or military)* list series, grade or rank, and, if promoted in this job, the date of your last promotion
Name	Area Code	Telephone No.		

Description of work: Describe your specific duties, responsibilities and accomplishments in this job, **including** the job title(s) of any employees you supervised. *If you describe more than one type of work (for example, carpentry and painting, or personnel and budget), write the approximate percentage of time you spent doing each.*

For Agency Use (skill codes, etc.)

☐ Name and address of employer's organization *(include ZIP Code, if known)*	Dates employed *(give month, day and year)*	Average number of hours per week	Number of employees you supervised
	From: To:		
	Salary or earnings	Your reason for leaving	
	Starting $ per		
	Ending $ per		

Your immediate supervisor			Exact title of your job	If Federal employment *(civilian or military)* list series, grade or rank, and, if promoted in this job, the date of your last promotion
Name	Area Code	Telephone No.		

Description of work: Describe your specific duties, responsibilities and accomplishments in this job, **including** the job title(s) of any employees you supervised. *If you describe more than one type of work (for example, carpentry and painting, or personnel and budget), write the approximate percentage of time you spent doing each.*

For Agency Use (skill codes, etc.)

THE FEDERAL GOVERNMENT IS AN EQUAL OPPORTUNITY EMPLOYER

PREVIOUS EDITION USABLE

Standard Form 171-A (Rev. 6-88)
U.S. Office of Personnel Management
FPM Chapter 295

Form Approved
OMB No. 3206-0219

OPTIONAL APPLICATION FOR FEDERAL EMPLOYMENT - OF 612

You may apply for most jobs with a resume, this form, or other written format. If your resume or application does not provide all the information requested on this form and in the job vacancy announcement, you may lose consideration for a job.

1 Job title in announcement

2 Grade(s) applying for

3 Announcement number

4 Last name   First and middle names

5 Social Security Number

6 Mailing address

City   State   ZIP Code

7 Phone numbers (include area code)
Daytime
Evening

WORK EXPERIENCE

8 Describe your paid and nonpaid work experience related to the job for which you are applying. Do **not** attach job descriptions.

1) Job title (if Federal, include series and grade)

From (MM/YY)   To (MM/YY)   Salary $ per   Hours per week

Employer's name and address

Supervisor's name and phone number

Describe your duties and accomplishments

2) Job title (if Federal, include series and grade)

From (MM/YY)   To (MM/YY)   Salary $ per   Hours per week

Employer's name and address

Supervisor's name and phone number

Describe your duties and accomplishments

GENERAL INFORMATION

9 May we contact your current supervisor?

YES [   ]   NO [   ]▶ If we need to contact your current supervisor before making an offer, we will contact you first.

EDUCATION

10 Mark highest level completed. **Some HS** [   ] **HS/GED** [   ] **Associate** [   ] **Bachelor** [   ] **Master** [   ] **Doctoral** [   ]

11 Last high school (HS) or GED school. Give the school's name, city, State, ZIP Code (if known), and year diploma or GED received.

12 Colleges and universities attended. Do **not** attach a copy of your transcript unless requested.

Name		Total Credits Earned Semester Quarter	Major(s)	Degree - Year (if any) Received
1)				
City	State ZIP Code			
2)				
3)				

OTHER QUALIFICATIONS

13 **Job-related** training courses (give title and year). **Job-related** skills (other languages, computer software/hardware, tools, machinery, typing speed, etc.). **Job-related** certificates and licenses (current only). **Job-related** honors, awards, and special accomplishments (publications, memberships in professional/honor societies, leadership activities, public speaking, and performance awards). Give dates, but do **not** send documents unless requested.

GENERAL

14 Are you a U.S. citizen?   **YES** [   ]   **NO** [   ]▶ Give the country of your citizenship.

15 Do you claim veterans' preference? **NO** [   ]   **YES** [   ]▶ Mark your claim of 5 or 10 points below.
  5 points [   ]▶ Attach your DD 214 or other proof. **10 points** [   ]▶ Attach an *Application for 10-Point Veterans' Preference* (SF 15) and proof required.

16 Were you ever a Federal civilian employee?   Series   Grade   From (MM/YY)   To (MM/YY)
  NO [   ] **YES** [   ]▶ For highest civilian grade give:

17 Are you eligible for reinstatement based on career or career-conditional Federal status?
  NO [   ] **YES** [   ]▶ If requested, attach SF 50 proof.

APPLICANT CERTIFICATION

18 **I certify** that, to the best of my knowledge and belief, all of the information on and attached to this application is true, correct, complete and made in good faith. **I understand** that false or fraudulent information on or attached to this application may be grounds for not hiring me or for firing me after I begin work, and may be punishable by fine or imprisonment. **I understand** that any information I give may be investigated.

SIGNATURE   DATE SIGNED